Mentoring Digital Media Projects

Project-Based Learning and Teaching for Professional Development

Patrick Parra Pennefather

Apress®

Mentoring Digital Media Projects: Project-Based Learning and Teaching for Professional Development

Patrick Parra Pennefather
Vancouver, BC, Canada

ISBN-13 (pbk): 978-1-4842-8797-2   ISBN-13 (electronic): 978-1-4842-8798-9
https://doi.org/10.1007/978-1-4842-8798-9

Copyright © 2022 by Patrick Parra Pennefather

Managing Director, Apress Media LLC: Welmoed Spahr
Acquisitions Editor: James Robinson-Prior
Development Editor: James Markham
Coordinating Editor: Gryffin Winkler

Cover image designed by eStudioCalamar

Distributed to the book trade worldwide by Springer Science+Business Media New York, 233 Spring Street, 6th Floor, New York, NY 10013. Phone 1-800-SPRINGER, fax (201) 348-4505, e-mail orders-ny@springer-sbm.com, or visit www.springeronline.com. Apress Media, LLC is a California LLC and the sole member (owner) is Springer Science + Business Media Finance Inc (SSBM Finance Inc). SSBM Finance Inc is a **Delaware** corporation.

For information on translations, please e-mail booktranslations@springernature.com; for reprint, paperback, or audio rights, please e-mail bookpermissions@springernature.com.

Apress titles may be purchased in bulk for academic, corporate, or promotional use. eBook versions and licenses are also available for most titles. For more information, reference our Print and eBook Bulk Sales web page at http://www.apress.com/bulk-sales.

Any source code or other supplementary material referenced by the author in this book is available to readers on GitHub.

Printed on acid-free paper

Table of Contents

About the Author

 **Patrick Parra Pennefather** is an Assistant Professor at the University of British Columbia within the Faculty of Arts and Faculty in Residence at the Emerging Media Lab. His research is focused on collaborative learning practices, digital media, sound design, mixed reality, and Agile software development. Patrick also works with learning organizations and technology companies around the world to design learning that meets the needs of diverse communities to aid the development of the next generation of technology designers and developers.

Patrick has mentored over 300 graduate and undergraduate students on 45 real-world projects with client partners from the gaming, xR, arts, web development and not-for profit communities of practice.

About the Technical Reviewers

 **Larry Bafia** is an animator and educator who works with various media. Larry started his career in stop motion and claymation with Crocus Productions in Chicago and then the Will Vinton Studios in Portland, Oregon. At the Vinton studio for nearly a decade, Larry worked on stop motion projects such as the California Raisins and Michael Jackson's Moonwalker. During a seven-year stint as Commercial Animation Director at PDI/ DreamWorks, Larry directed commercials for many top clients including Coca-Cola, Sega, Intel, Kraft, Target, Circle K, and Saturn. As an active member of the SIGGRAPH Conference Committee, Larry has chaired the 2018 Computer Animation Festival, the 2019 Creative Development Team, and the 2021 VR Theater.

From 2002 through 2008, Larry was Department Head of Animation and Visual Effects at the Vancouver Film School. Larry has also served as VP of Faculty and Development at VanArts as well as the Director of the Master of Digital Media Program at the Centre for Digital Media, Vancouver, BC.

Kimberly Voll is a designer, developer, and researcher passionate about digital social dynamics, the future of interaction, and how we can thrive together in online spaces. In 2017, Kim cofounded the Fair Play Alliance (FPA), a global coalition of today over 250 gaming companies united in improving development practices to foster healthy, inclusive gaming spaces. In addition to helping run the FPA, she is currently a Studio Head at Brace Yourself Games and is a longtime game maker. Kim also spent several years at Riot Games as a principal technical game designer and as the Head of Player Dynamics, as well as independently launching several indie projects, including Fantastic Contraption for VR. She holds a PhD in computer science (AI) and honors degree in cognitive science.

Introduction

A colleague I met at SXSW many years ago from the mobile game industry called me up from Austin and after short hellos asked: "Hey, I know you've been teaching digital projects for a while and I'm wondering if you have any tips 'cause I've been asked to teach a course in the fall?" Like any designer, who is approached with a design problem, dozens of questions popped up in my mind. "Who's the course for? What are you teaching them? What department? Skillsets? Duration of course? How many hours per week? Teach game-making?" Why this now? I visualized a mind map that became filled with these questions. How could I organize all of that in a simple response? I had only been teaching for about eight years so what did I know? They're asking and I'm stumbling for the order of words I should speak first. "Well," I replied, with a long pause. "Let me think out loud." Then the answers started to pour out, and after about what felt like a good ten minutes, my colleague interrupted. "Well now. I got some of that. Can you send the rest in an email?"

I sent off bullet points and my colleague found some of what they could decipher useful. That email became the foundation for a book that you now have in front of you. It has taken a while to write it because like many people, it's hard to find the time to write down what you know that would be helpful to others in your communities of practice who might benefit.

Why this book now?

The best answer arises from a comment that a colleague in the games industry in Vancouver made many years ago that still echoes today. "They're just not coming in with enough know-how to learn what they need to get the job done fast enough." There's a lot to unpack with that statement. If you relate to this at all, it's because it is a common theme that has been repeated for well over a century. It reveals a persistent disconnect between the skills and competencies that employers in the digital media industry and beyond need to thrive and survive, with the training that is lacking across the offerings of public and private post-secondary institutions. Many educators, government officials, and employers in the service and resource industries at all levels of influence are aware of the problem and champion new approaches to solving it.

Learning by Doing As a Solution

Historically, scholars refer to the early writings and influence of American pragmatist John Dewey and his thoughts on "Progressive Education" to discuss the benefits of *learning by doing*. It's important to know that there are many themes in Dewey's writing on education including the following:

- There is great value in giving students embodied experiences of learning instead of passively absorbing knowledge and regurgitating it when tested.

- Students learn more from reflecting on their experience of learning than from the experience of learning alone.

- Learning how to learn is just as important as learning a subject and should be a part of every curriculum that is taught.

- In any educational environment, students should have a voice, where they can interact with the curriculum and make choices as to what would most benefit them to learn.

One of his lesser-known quotes is one relevant and provoking, therefore worthy of sharing here.

"If we teach today's students as we taught yesterday's, we rob them of tomorrow."

The disconnect between what is taught and what is expected from the digital media industry is common and many professional programs have emerged to address the need, one of which I had the privilege of getting off the ground with others from the digital media industry. Yet, the demand keeps growing and shifting for relevant educational experiences that address the needs of today, and institutions just cannot keep up with the rapidly changing demands. Bear in mind, this has been a constant historical struggle. New initiatives like microcredential programs have surfaced to fill needed gaps, and to offer retraining to existing employees, because many work environments are increasingly requiring skills and competencies as they transform to integrate the use and development of digital solutions for their customers. Microcredentials are attractive because they are "lighter." In some cases, they require less bureaucracy to get off the ground and are smaller and shorter in duration than a typical 12-week course. They offer an extension of knowledge to those who already have a foundation and they are ideally targeted to self-regulating learners, those who have the competency to manage their own learning process.

This book adds to a body of knowledge that has roots in the past while trying to stay ever relevant to designs of learning that will most benefit students wanting to work in the digital media industry. It is an extension of Dewey's pragmatic vision of learning by doing, an ever-adaptive framework that can be applied to the practice of teaching and mentoring project-based courses in post-secondary learning environments. It is intended to support the pragmatist in each of us who wants to design, teach, and mentor courses that emphasize learning by doing.

If you are drawn to creating a course like this, or have been asked to, and you happen to come from a profession that is embedded in the digital media industry, you are at an advantage. You are used to learning by doing as that is an essential feature of developing emerging technologies. How to design a course that champions learning by doing in an academic environment is not entirely clear for many professionals who have an impulse to want to teach. That impulse may be motivated by having the experience of witnessing recruits who want their dream job in your work environment, but who don't have the types of skills and competencies to successfully transition, or who become overly reliant on others to ramp up what they need to know to perform their jobs well. The tools and strategies this book offer will also be helpful for those who want to design a more robust learning pipeline in their workplace and may help identify some of the gaps in know-how that a recruit will have as they begin their job in your company.

To be clear, there is no foolproof starting point for the adventure of guiding students to build emerging technology projects in post-secondary. Coming from a highly collaborative digital media industry, you have learned from and mentored others in the workplace. If you are like most professionals I know, you probably didn't write down what worked and what didn't because you likely didn't have the luxury of time to do that. There is, however, a path for you to get there. Admittedly, it is a bit of a windy path yes, but each of the chapters in this book addresses the interconnected elements that will support you in designing, teaching, and mentoring a project-based course. The learning outcomes of that course aim to help students to intentionally develop 21st century competencies that will accelerate their transition into a highly collaborative digital media workplace.

Consider this book a helpful companion that you can open and find useful tools and approaches inside of, as you extend your expertise into facilitating post-secondary learning environments. It will be useful for those who want to teach and mentor projects in post-secondary settings no matter what their profession in the digital media industry. Digital media projects cover a wide range of media. They can be in interactive web dev, mobile game, 2D and 3D animation, mobile application development, use of machine learning or xR (virtual, augmented, headset augmented, and mixed reality), NFT creation, interactive 360 video, or whatever experiences the latest up and coming technology will offer us. The approaches to designing teaching and mentoring that are described in this book are intended to build from the mentoring practice you already have developed in the workplace. The book is designed to help you identify and organize the knowledge and experience you have gained that can support learners on digital media projects across formal learning environments.

The book draws from my own patterns of teaching and mentoring over 45 projects for the past 15 years at the Master of Digital Media Program and at the University of British Columbia in Vancouver, Canada. The approach to designing learning also comes from mentoring the mentor to design learning interactions with students in graduate and undergraduate technology projects. In addition, the book will draw from previously conducted methods, development pipelines, and research on mentoring in post-secondary environments that mentors can use to design their own teaching and mentoring. It supports professionals to design a learning pipeline, teach, and mentor students who are developing emerging technology within different types of learning environments.

Book Objectives

After reading this book you will:

- Acquire a solid foundation for designing teaching and mentoring interactions in an undergraduate or graduate course focused on team-based emerging technology development

- Identify your own teaching and mentoring strategies and apply these within a project-based learning pipeline

- Design a project-based course with learning outcomes that include 21st-century competencies and the criteria through which to assess them

How to Read This Book

When you want to learn something new and you're busy, you go for what's essential. This book is perfect for the busy. Besides, when it comes to teaching and mentoring how to guide people and teach what they need on emerging technology projects, it's important to get to what you think you need the most quickly. When it comes to learning how to teach and mentor in different learning environments, there can be a lot to learn and no right order to learn things in. This book is structured to help get you to what you need quickly without necessarily having to read what came before.

Chapter 1 gives you some theory to navigate the territory of project-based learning. This is useful to ground your learning outcomes in what has come before.

Chapters 2 and 3 support you to think about your own workplace mentoring strategies and how your mentor will act as a ringmaster for what you think needs to be taught, and in the design of activities students engage in that will need mentoring.

Chapters 4 and 5 distinguish between what you'll teach in a project-based course and what you'll mentor. This will also be emphasized by revealing some interaction patterns that are common in project courses.

Chapter 6 presents mentoring strategies drawn from research so you start to think about ones you've used in the workplace that might be effective in a project course.

Chapter 7 proposes features of PjBL to consider as you start to design activities and consider the competencies you want learners to leave the course with.

Chapter 8 helps you understand a typical project-based production pipeline giving you an overall template of a 12-week course with week-by-week breakdowns.

Chapter 9 draws your attention to differentiating between skills and competencies, so you can develop learning outcomes. The process in this chapter will eventually help you to create criteria as to how you'll assess learners giving you all the building blocks for a course outline.

Chapter 10 consists of a short conclusion and story.

The What, Why, and How of This Book

What: A book for professionals from the digital media industry who want to design, teach, and mentor a project-based course at a post-secondary institution.

Why: To give them a process to better understand what will be required of them when they transfer their knowledge and know-how to formal learning environments.

How: By providing a rich description of the environment they will teach in, some research to draw from, tools, approaches, frameworks, templates, instructional design methods, and use cases on the design of project courses focused on the development of emerging technologies.

Structure of Each Chapter

Each chapter starts with the chapter goal followed by a needs statement. That statement is influenced by user stories and statements common to Agile software development that describe an identified user and/or show a feature they might want and why it might benefit them. Mentor stories will be in a slightly different format and use "you" in their format.

To: (will identify the action)

You need: (will identify a feature in the book that will benefit you)

So you can: (will detail the outcome of learning what's in the chapter)

Each chapter will include tools and approaches to help deepen your mentoring practice and provide you with sufficient tools to design a project-based course by the end of the book.

Chapters have the same structured conclusions including a bullet point summary of what was covered in the chapter, tools and approaches that were proposed, and a Deeper Dive area suggesting more readings for those who want go deeper with any of the topics discussed in the chapter.

Now that the reasoning for this book along with its objectives has been explained, the next few chapters will guide you through the territory of project-based learning (PjBL), suggest you reflect and map out your approaches to mentoring, and help you understand your various roles that you'll play within a PjBL environment. Before that, a glossary of terms is presented to accelerate your understanding of terms that are used in the chapters to come.

Glossary

The following terms repeat quite a bit throughout the book. They are not in alphabetical order.

PjBL: An acronym for project-based learning. Why not PBL you might ask? Because it has already been used for many years standing for problem-based learning. Nevertheless, you may find books and articles that use PBL to describe project-based learning.

Learner: A pseudonym for student. Both words are interchanged in the novel. The term learner is more common on the ed tech theoretical and research literature.

Agile: Agile vs. agility here speaking to a project management methodology whose characteristics are useful particularly when adapted to the needs of a team.

Scrum: An important ritual in for Agile teams describing a three-part process of catching up with each other's work since team-based work is interdependent Scrum helps to identify obstacles that team members may need support in removing so they can continue development.

Sprint: In Agile there are short cycles of development where teams have a goal to co-construct as many features as they can within the defined period of time. Sprints recur and consist of a Retrospective where work done is reviewed and that review influences the next Sprint.

Epic: Not as commonly used, an Epic is a collection of sprints that lead to an integration point or as is more commonly used, a milestone. Project-based courses can be divided into two Epics with midterm evaluations as a middle milestone.

Backlog: In Agile processes work that is not complete ends up in the backlog. It's a place on the Scrum Board where tasks or features not complete end up. At the end of a Sprint, teams can then decide what they want to do with those tasks and/or features, prioritize them or deprioritize them, and then decide if they make it into the next Sprint.

User stories: User stories are a helpful story-based visual map to help teams define features of a project while keeping user's needs top of mind. Identifying a user first and their needs is followed by what they can achieve by fulfilling that need. Each User Story is usually associated with a feature.

xR: The acronym has multiple meanings in that it points to various types of media that offer users a different reality other than their commonly shared in-person one. Extended Reality is generally an umbrella term encompassing virtual, augmented, and mixed-reality experiences.

Fidelity: Used to describe a prototype by the degree to which it represents the original intent or idea. Low-fidelity prototypes are usually paper or physical prototypes, Higher fidelity ones tend to be digital ones.

Developer: Programmers are often referred to as developers on teams.

Wizard of Oz prototypes: These types of prototypes involve multiple methods and techniques to help a team fake interaction that they might yet have had time to co-construct.

Mixed reality: Mixed reality refers to the merging of our in-person reality with a mediated reality like mobile or headset augmented, or virtual reality. There are many different types, for example, using VR in combination with projection where experiences in VR can be seen on the screen and people outside of VR can also have their motion detected through sensors, appearing transformed within VR.

UX: Short for user experience, considering the UX tasks teams to always think of the user they are designing something for. This has become so important that individuals are hired and their sole job is to design the user experience.

Human-centered design: The term has become more meaningful and resonant with design teams to always consider the human in whatever they design. Teams however interchange user experience design with human-centered design.

Deliverable: That final prototype in whatever state it is in forms part of what is "delivered" to a client. This can include a working version of the prototype, documentation, code, art, and other assets.

Iterative: A term that describes a process where versions of prototypes are developed in cycles, usually at increasing levels of fidelity.

Proof of concept: A type of prototype, a representation that is intended to consist of the minimal amount of features to give people a good idea of the project.

Feature: Some type of essential component of a prototype. When grouped together, features contribute to the user experience of a prototype. A feature can be decomposed into tasks that make one up.

Dependency: Teams depend on each other to complete features by estimating how long it takes them to complete interdependent tasks.

Self-regulating: A term in this book and the literature it draws from to refer to a process where students manage their own learning, including all the related actions students need to engage in such as self-motivation, self-reliance, and self-management.

CHAPTER 1

Know the Territory: Learning Interactions in Project-Based Environments

Chapter Goal: This chapter identifies the types of learning interactions that occur on project-based courses. It dives into the foundations of project-based learning (PjBL) environments touching on the core features of PjBL, the types of learning interactions that occur, and the multiple types of roles that instructors play and how students learn. This chapter reveals the balance between teaching and mentoring when guiding learners on emerging technology project development. It charts known unknowns and unknown unknowns that readily occur within project-based courses that explains why mentoring is a key role that instructors will play.

To teach in a post-secondary learning environment

You need to understand some theory and research in PjBL

So you can have the rationale for the learning that you design and understand the multiple roles you will play when facilitating learners.

© Patrick Parra Pennefather 2022
P. Parra Pennefather, *Mentoring Digital Media Projects*,
https://doi.org/10.1007/978-1-4842-8798-9_1

*A creature ferrying a scholar across a turbulent river said
something ungrammatical to them. "Have you studied gram-
mar?" asked the scholar. "No", grumbled the beast. "Then half
of your life has been wasted." A few minutes later the creature
turned to the passenger startling them. "Have you ever learned
how to swim?", they growled. "No", replied the scholar. "Then
all your life is wasted – we are sinking!"*

(Revised Sufi tale, unknown source)

Foundations of Project-Based Learning

If you are new to taking on teaching a course in a more formal learning
environment, then you might feel a bit like that creature, ferrying learners
across the at-times turbulent and unknown waters of project-based
learning (PjBL). Rest assured though that PjBL is so different than most
learning environments that even accomplished teachers who have never
taught it before can feel uncomfortable and uneasy when they attempt
to take it on. It demands a lot from the instructor and the learner. It is
helpful then to know that there are some common characteristics to PjBL
environments.

Common Characteristics

Collaborative project-based learning with real-world projects in a learning
environment include the following common characteristics that can be
referenced in the research and theoretical literature that spans the last
40 years:

- Activities are centered around solving problems
  through prototyping.

- Identifying problems to solve in a design process sometimes emerges from the act of prototyping.

- Learners solve problems together with a constant negotiation of their individual impulses.

- They learn not just about how to solve problems, but how they individually contribute to solving them.

- The process of solving a problem is more important than the solution itself.

- The process of solving problems demands that the learner draw on previous knowledge and is also comfortable uncovering unknown knowledge.

- The unknown knowledge students need to acquire is like a piece of a puzzle not yet found, or a handful of puzzle pieces that learners need to try to fit together to determine if they really fit.

- The process of solving problems can engage a learner's curiosity, frustration, and the desire for the mind to propose an ongoing series of solutions.

- Team members are challenged to adapt to new kinds of peer relationships.

- Learners are persistently assessed based not solely on what they contribute to a conversation or in the completion of an assignment but how they work with others to identify and solve problems in the form of prototypes.

- The design encourages students to learn much of what they need to learn, on their own and from each other.

- Teaching and mentoring interactions focus on facilitating learners to self-regulate or manage their own learning experience while co-constructing digital prototypes.

- Key learning outcomes are matched with competencies learners need to have as they transition into related communities of practice.

Teaching and Learning Interactions in PjBL

Project-based courses are at times misunderstood within academic institutions as courses where students just make stuff. That misunderstanding persists among some academics as if it were a lower form of learning that is somehow lacking in content, critical thinking, rigor, or designed learning outcomes. Those misconceptions are far from the truth. PjBL encompasses all other forms of teaching, such as traditional lecture-based learning, group discussion and problem solving, synchronous and asynchronous activities, and unplanned microlearning sessions as interventions that culminate in a type of capstone or final course project. One of the differences from other types of learning is that activities in a PjBL course are centered around learning all the requirements necessary for students to create a project together that is suitable to the time requirements of the course and that require specific skills they may not yet possess. Centering all learning activities around co-constructing a tangible artifact may sound like simply following the instructions to build a model ship, but if you come from any type of professional industry, being able to navigate others to do so can feel more like building the ship while sailing unknown waters and trying to keep a team staying afloat.

Roles That Instructors Play in PjBL

Managing student teams requires resilience and ability to thrive under pressure that has likely contributed to your own success in the workplace. It requires a similar approach in the workplace that is supportive of fellow workers to make goals, strive for excellence, and remove obstacles to ensure success. Given that PjBL involves different ways of learning, an instructor must be prepared to wear several hats including that of instructional designer, teacher, group facilitator, content creator, conflict resolver, industry advisor, coach, producer, and of course, mentor.

One of those hats an instructor wears is as a mentor, which is an effective and commonly reported interaction between learners and instructors. Those with experience mentoring teams on emerging technology projects in industry have an advantage in understanding many of the challenges learners will face, compared to those who have never had that lived experience. There is no question that the lived experience of supervising and mentoring individuals on your team qualifies you to share expertise at a university level. This includes what you've had to learn to contribute to project development, the research you've undertaken to improve team performance, management practices, the innovation you may have engaged in, culture and productivity, and the results of those efforts as a published work.

How Students Learn in PjBL

Students need to be guided to learn in a variety of different ways, some of which may not be familiar to them. Figure 1-1 summarizes some of the ways that students learn in a PjBL environment.

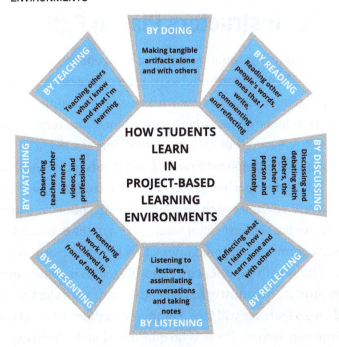

Figure 1-1. *Different ways that students learn in PjBL environments*

By Doing

In much of the literature on PjBL, there is a persistent description of
how people learn. The dominant manner is by "doing." To be clear, when
learners engage in other forms of instruction, they are still actively doing
something, whether that something is listening, taking notes, reading, or
conversing with other learners and/or the instructor. In PjBL, however,
doing is an act of creation. The active verb describes a process through
which students gain know-how by fulfilling specific tasks related to
project development. Directly and in the case of emerging technology
development, this can mean contributing to a project with the creation
of 3D or 2D art assets. It can also mean coding interactions if you are
a programmer, designing the user interface if you are a UI designer,

managing the project if you are a project manager, etc. The process of
learning by doing occurs when learners are tasked to create emerging
technology together. While engaged in the act of fulfilling tasks they are
assigned to, which contribute to a group project, they also come across
limitations of their knowledge and know-how and must also learn what
they need to stretch beyond their limited know-how.

Compare the process of learning how to play the piano. You can learn
about the piano through books and listening. You can learn about the
social history of the piano, its role in society, and the music played on it
over centuries since its invention. You can learn the theory that influenced
how different types of piano music were composed in different musical
eras. You can even learn to read piano music. However, the only way to
learn how to play the piano is to play it. Then and only then is the mind
and body fully engaged in the act of bringing it to life. The other ways of
learning the piano may help support the actual playing of the instrument.
Playing the piano means developing technique, which when applied to
piano music develops the player's craft. The complexity of what piano
compositions that a pianist can play is interdependent on their practice of
the technique required to exercise the muscles, dexterity and coordination
of the fingers, hands, and body. Once the inherent technique required
to play Chopin's Fantaisie-Impromptu in C# minor is embodied through
reading the music while playing it, it can be memorized without the need
to read the music, as long as the piece of music is persistently practiced.
Where the budding piano player has an advantage over a student learning
how to develop an emerging technology is that the instrument exists, as
does the piece of music (at least in classical piano music). The student in
a PjBL environment is prototyping the piano, the music, and user testing
how it will best be played.

By Reading

In PjBL, learners must be able to read texts that support them in deepening their understanding of co-constructing projects with others. They read everything from research articles to blog posts and book excerpts to understand the territory, learn what others have done before to solve problems they might encounter, and dissect specific knowledge from the most recent documentation available on a shared code repository to understand how previous code and the coding process can help them with their current undertaking. Reading is directed toward improving their understanding of the project co-constructive process and is less about reading philosophies about project creation than it is about reading documented practice to support their own practice. Those readings are also intended to give students use cases they can compare their work to. It's comforting to sometimes read about stories of failure from veterans in the digital media industry when you are starting out yourself. Students need to understand that everyone struggles, and that the development of new technology is not easy.

By Teaching

There are multiple occasions where students learn from each other. The best teams are those where individuals share knowledge with others as they are engaged in co-constructing projects together. PjBL acknowledges the value of individual differences and can leverage the knowledge and experience that each person brings to the process of collaborative creation. Learners on teams must also present to the whole class on what they've learned while engaging in the co-construction of a project. This back-and-forth knowledge sharing between individuals and teams creates a healthy ecosystem where the instructor is no longer seen as the center of knowledge. This is important as it speaks to one of the outcomes of PjBL, which is to empower learners to self-regulate.

By Watching

By watching and observing experts, students can then apply technique
and approach to their own projects. This is achieved through a variety of
media that exists to support everything from how to contend with collision
of objects in a specific game environment like Unreal to how to manage
tasks on an Agile Scrum board. Careful observation of one another during
any team meetings is also how students learn to be discerning and how
they develop and sustain their own developing practices. Finally, watching
the presentation of works in progress or prototypes from other teams
challenges learners to focus their attention in the moment, particularly if
feedback from those observing is elicited in Q&A afterward.

By Discussing

There is plenty of discussion that occurs during any emerging tech
pipeline. Learners actively engage in discussion that is centered around
creative solutions to problems, collaboration, and communication.
Discussion tends to be focused on supporting their combined efforts
to create prototypes and define the user experience of what they
are designing. By articulating their thoughts, students share their
understanding of every aspect of the PjBL pipeline.

By Presenting

In PjBL environments, tasking learners to persistently (weekly) present
their ideas, share their assignments, and report on project process is a
strategic way to challenge them to improve how they articulate their ideas.
This can be amplified through feedback sessions that follow. Instructors
can elicit feedback that has directly to do with how individuals on teams
articulated their ideas. Guiding learners in this way can help them be more
articulate in how they share their ideas.

By Reflecting

Through regular feedback cycles, students are challenged to reflect
on the work they co-create in addition to the process of creation itself.
Regularly embedded reflective tools will increase learner awareness and
allow them to check in on earlier made goals, adjust performance, and
when necessary fine-tune their behaviors to one another. Agile teams that
improve over time take the time to conduct Retrospectives at the end of a
Sprint or cycle of time. These types of reflective activities remind learners
that they may be going through similar challenges that others are and
provide multiple opportunities to affirm and be affirmed for their efforts.

By Listening

Along with discussion, students learn by listening to short lectures and
presentations by other students and student teams and during project
group work. Practicing listening is an important part of a communicative
project team, and it will benefit your students to embed different types of
listening activities so they can become increasingly aware as to how they
communicate with one another through active listening and discussion.

   While students learn in many ways as detailed earlier, they also learn
in surprising ways. This is because engaging in the co-construction of
projects can lead to as many known knowns, as there are unforeseen or
unknown situations.

Chart the Known Knowns and the Known Unknowns of PjBL in Post-secondary

*"Known unknowns result from phenomena which are recog-
nized, but poorly understood."*

(Report from BC Mining, Canada, 1979)

There are those things we can come to expect and those we cannot when implementing a project-based course in post-secondary settings. This is like a workplace environment where teams engage in creating something new or innovative. In many business settings, the language of a pivot or the practice of pivoting is commonly used to describe the need for an individual, team, or company to shift directions due to unforeseen circumstances. At times, pivots are expected. These are known unknowns because we can accept that they will occur, we recognize them when they do, but we don't really understand them fully or what shape they'll take. Understanding the known unknowns that will more than likely occur in PjBL environments can at least prepare you to mitigate them ahead of time, should they arise. It's always good to have a backup plan.

Of course, through experience and the literature on developing projects in educational environments, we can similarly plot known knowns. The following known knowns dominantly come from the experience of engaging in project development across different types of projects, students, clients, and learning environments. Identifying known knowns leads to insights on how to design "features" of project-based learning that students will benefit from. These include the following:

- Projects tend to be motivated by a problem to solve that is not always based on supporting or sustaining a business.

- Projects tend to be small in scope compared to a project in industry because students are not "full-time" in the same way, and they are learning their craft and how to apply it with others simultaneously.

- Students mainly learn by "doing." Differently from how they learn in a lecture though, the "doing" is centered around making something. They apply their craft and

work together with others to create tangible prototypes
and artifacts that culminate in a finished "product."

- Those who facilitate PjBL environments tend to spend
most of their time mentoring students, that is, in
guiding them toward self-managing what they need to
learn to complete a project vs. teaching them specific
skills (drawing, coding, how to design).

The final known known of PjBL is that it is easy enough to predict that
unexpected or unknown events will occur that learners will have to face
and resolve.

Known Unknowns of PjBL Environments

Generalizing research undertaken in PjBL environments that can help
us design a project-based course is somewhat useful, but there is some
difficulty in drawing from a single project because every project is
different, including how the project is managed, how much time learners
have to work on it, what technology is being developed, and how much
time a mentor needs to spend with the team.

For example, even though we might know the mechanics of how a
project management methodology may be applied to a specific project,
we don't really know what will transpire when it is applied by a specific
set of learners. The factors that distinguish one project from another
will influence how Agile is applied. Teaching the principles of Agile is a
known known. The benefits of applying many of the principles of Agile
are numerous including its capacity to adapt to any type of collaborative
project that learners might take on.

That said, *how* Agile ends up being adopted and integrated by a team
is a known unknown. Like Agile, there are many more core features of PjBL
that can be considered known unknowns. Figure 1-2 details several of
these known unknowns that will influence your design; what, when, and

how much you teach; and the balance between teaching and mentoring within a PjBL course focused on emerging technology development. These are considerations to consider as you begin to think about teaching a course in a more formal learning environment.

Figure 1-2. *Some of the KNOWN UNKNOWNS when designing and implementing a PjBL course*

Team

The team makeup and the skills that students bring to a project influence what is possible. It's difficult to know with complete certainty what will make a good project or a client for that matter when you are not even aware of the skills that learners have. You also get what you get and you don't know what that will be until your first class. Unlike industry, you can't hire external learners to make up for a lack of skills on a team. The aesthetic of learners is also unknown challenging you to pick projects that are broader in appeal. You don't really know what project a student will gravitate toward and so giving them choice and balancing how a team is composed vs. student wants is unpredictable. If it is a project with a client partner, then ensuring they too are flexible with what the project becomes is important to keep in mind. This is because students often lack experience with project development and arrive ill-equipped to assess a way forward when they are faced with a problem.

How teams apply the specific tools that you introduce is unknown. As much as you might know how well certain tools work in your own practice, their successful application is often determined by how they are applied and if their function is understood. They will likely be unclear when to apply tools that you model. It is often difficult for students to understand their purpose because they don't have the same experience of applying the tool across a production pipeline. What can be expected is that students will either apply tools you propose, adapt them, or they'll come up with their own. Which tools they end up finding the most useful for the situation is unknown when you first start out teaching a PjBL course. Facilitating an understanding of how tools are applied in industry is another way to help them understand their use.

Medium

The type of technology students will be developing and how it might relate to a particular community of practice is another known unknown. This is because if you challenge them to solve a problem through the development of technology, it is hard to tell if Virtual Reality, Augmented Reality, or another emerging technology will solve the problem the team and the client partner are attempting to identify and solve. Because of this, you will need to draw from expertise in the communities of practice you engage with, should students need more media-specific support than you are able to provide.

Access to equipment including powerful enough computers for students to complete their tasks may be known or a known unknown as enrollment numbers will influence budget. What you can't predict is if students who enroll have a powerful enough computer to handle emerging tech development, particularly if they want to use a game engine. So how can this be resolved? One solution is to partner with an existing lab, library, or department unit that might provide you access.

Project

How long students remain within the phases of a project pipeline is unknown. While a carved out PjBL pipeline is proposed in Chapter 7, it is meant to be an adaptable template. You'll never really be able to tell just how much time a student team will need at the different phases of production. This might impact the overall class progression influencing everything from intended learning outcomes to the final project deliverable.

The personality, work habits, and experience of the client partner if there is an external client can be unknown especially if you haven't worked with them in the context of interfacing with students. Client relationships need to be managed and expectations of their involvement in a course need to be communicated up front, and if helpful, a signed agreement will help. Learners need clients particularly in the opening weeks of the project to ensure they are reading a brief correctly, checking in for changes, and confirming the features and the project itself. They need clients to give them feedback and to approve choices. Clients can easily fade after the initial excitement of kickoff, so planning a weekly meetup with remote communication in between classes is advised. Despite all the mitigation strategies you apply, however, you still cannot predict how the relationship between client, learner, and you will evolve.

Mentor

How much experience you have had developing emerging technologies is a known unknown for the course and the students. It is difficult to say whether less or more experience on production pipelines influence how well students receive your teaching and mentoring. Some of that is also dependent on the role(s) you played on those production teams. The varied types of experiences that you bring to a PjBL course will support you and learners when obstacles show up or problems occur. That said, you can't predict them all. There's nothing wrong in curating people with more experience to occasionally visit or provide feedback to the learners. Strategically, it makes learners feel a bit more connected to the local industry around them.

How much mentoring support you will need to provide students and teams is a known unknown in PjBL courses. When considering taking on a PjBL course, schedule in time ahead of the course and understand when some weeks might be challenging. Planning ahead will guide the time that you spend with learners and the project, in addition to understanding the boundaries you might have. Regardless of what you plot out ahead of time, there will still be moments where you feel a team needs more support, particularly if you are as deeply invested in their success as they are. Thus, a known unknown will be the mentoring load you will experience.

The connection the mentor has to a specific community of practice that values the integration of emerging technologies to solve human problems will be different for each industry, and even within the same one. A connection to a community of practice allows mentors and students the possibility of accessing professionals in the community who may offer workshops, further mentorship, and advice to learners. It opens the course to allow for a diversity of voices expanding the knowledge of learners and affirming the messages the mentor is teaching. That said, every time you teach a PjBL course, the community has likely evolved. New emerging technologies also play a role in the design process as well as the priorities of a community of practice.

Having some type of teaching assistant or other human resource support throughout the course may be unknown at first. It might really depend on the number of learners enrolled. Having a TA is important in a PjBL course because things happen quickly, and you need another set of eyes on everything to increase how much time you can give learners. It's difficult to know how much time they'll need or how large a class will be until your first class so it will be helpful to account for students needing more time if you have less support than you anticipated.

Learner Response

How much time students are willing to spend developing the project regardless of the course credit value. This in turn will affect how many features a project can consist of. This factor makes the difference as to whether a course outcome is a proof-of-concept project or a more developed minimum viable product. While you may have a good idea of the course hours and the expected work learners undertake each week, you can never really estimate the level of involvement that learners will commit to.

It is impossible to know before you start and in some cases during a course if the learning outcomes associated with the project co-construction

process are being achieved by all students. Tying the competencies you
want learners to develop through targeted activities may be one way
to increase knowledge, and midsemester interviews can tell you a lot.
Ultimately though, in PjBL, many of the learning outcomes are tied to
the prototypes learners make and the process they undertake to
co-construct them.

Relying on learning outcomes based on research and/or previous
experience may be helpful but may need to be adjusted along the way.
Knowing the research done previously on PjBL will help guide you in
the first stages of designing your learning outcomes. Anticipate they will
need to be adjusted depending on what learners you have in the course
and what their learning goals are. Learning outcomes may need to be
calibrated accordingly.

These are just some of the known unknowns that will influence any
PjBL course focused on developing emerging technologies. Internal and
external factors influence how the course is designed. When you look
at the sum of all the factors you will need to consider prior to offering
a project-based course, you quickly realize that there is no one way,
how-to process, shortcut, or template that will work for every learning
environment, every course, or every student.

To Do: Map Known Knowns and Known Unknowns

It is useful to map the known knowns and known unknowns that you've
experienced managing or being part of teams in your own workplace. This
will help identify ones that may be more relevant to the PjBL environment
that you design. Use Figure 1-3 or something similar to map some known
knowns and known unknowns that you've experienced in the workplace
that might be applicable to a PjBL environment.

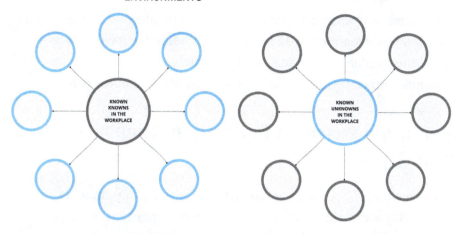

Figure 1-3. *Visual model can be used to brainstorm known
unknowns in the workplace that may map to a PjBL environment*

How PjBL Reinvents How Teachers and Learners Interact

Because of the seemingly overwhelming number of known unknowns
present in PjBL, and the various roles that instructors and learners play,
these types of learning environments force a rethink of the teaching and
learning interactions that students and instructors are more familiar with.
PjBL challenges the most dominant method of learning where a large
class of learners are expected to absorb facts, memorize the important
ones, and regurgitate them when they are tested. Facilitating learners
to co-construct projects in post-secondary institutions will be a bit of a
shock to learners used to that type of passive learning model. PjBL follows
a long history where instructor/learner relationships are not usually
recounted since little has been written about specific use cases that
occur across disciplines. More evidence-based research has been written
about the advantages of PjBL in Kindergarten to Grade 12 environments,

with authors advocating for the many benefits of integrating project and problem-based learning within courses. It is helpful to research some of the writing available at the end of this chapter, as generalizations that have been made might be applicable to post-secondary environments.

Mentoring Learners to Navigate Their Own Experiences

One of the most important affordances of PjBL is that it proposes an opportunity for instructors to mentor learners to manage their own learning goals, their collaborative relationships with each other, and all aspects of the project from inception to final deliverable. Instructors teach the tools that allow learners to manage these three intersecting characteristics of PjBL. They then mentor learners as these tools are applied to the project pipeline itself.

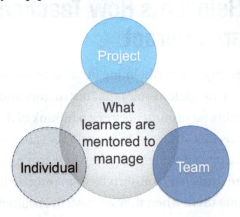

Figure 1-4. *Three areas students are mentored to manage within PjBL courses*

Project

To manage projects, students need to learn the basics. They need to understand project management, timeboxing, when a task is considered complete, and a feature done. They need to know what an appropriate scope of the project is and receive feedback so they can assess what is good enough. All these experiences cannot be understood through lecture alone. Students need to be guided experientially while undertaking tasks related to building a project together and be able to manage their and their client's expectations as well.

Individual

Assertions from research conducted within post-secondary institutions build on the many features of project courses and particularly on the capacity for PjBL to support self-regulation. Mentoring is key in supporting students to manage what they need to learn to deliver a project on time, with a limited set of features, and develop targeted competencies in the process. This is to the mentee's benefit as their propensity to manage themselves, their learning, their time, their own problem-solving processes in a variety of digital media work environments will have a direct impact on their value as central participants in an organization. Similar to supervising a doctoral student, the act of mentoring involves the capacity to assess where an individual is at, what they need support with, and what obstacles they may need support in removing. That assessment then leads to feedback that is actionable—in other words, feedback that will continue to support students in their ongoing development and improvement of whatever it is they are building.

Team

Teams are composed of individuals, all of whom have various levels of experience collaborating with other individuals. In terms of managing themselves as a team, there is much to learn in practice. This includes basics about how to forge aligned values, how to enact Rules of Play, best practices in collaboration, which include offering and sharing ideas openly, communicated work ethic, etc. Ultimately, mentoring a team to manage themselves without too much interference is one of the goals in PjBL courses. This is not achieved through traditional teaching or doctoral supervision as each individual is contributing to the same project. Mentoring teams requires a delicate balance between supporting individuals and supporting the team itself. It requires the discernment to differentiate what would most benefit the team and the project at any given moment during a production period.

Figure 1-5. *Mentoring self-regulation is one of the distinguishing actions that instructors of PjBL environments will engage in persistently*

Chapter Summary

Becoming increasingly aware as to how you mentor in the workplace will be important to reflect on and capture as you read the next chapter.

This chapter

- Introduced core features of a project-based learning (PjBL) environment

- Proposed that instructors relate to learners in multiple types of ways: through short lectures, demonstrations of tools, modelling an approach to design, and mentoring

- Described a common intent that instructors play in a PjBL environment to guide learners to manage themselves, the project, and a client partner

- Defined the potent combination of actions and approaches as mentoring

- Revealed that in PjBL learners are exposed to a different kind of learning experience, one that is more experiential where they learn by doing

- Suggested that learners will develop know-how applying the knowledge that you teach

- Explained that the known knowns and known unknowns of PjBL in the development of emerging technology are well matched to instructors experienced with project development pipelines

Tools and Suggested Processes

- Deepen understanding of common characteristics of PjBL.

- Be aware that there are different roles instructors play in PjBL environments.

- The way that students learn in PjBL can help provide variation in activities and assignments.

- Recognize there are known knowns and known unknowns in PjBL.

- Figure 1-4 shows three dominant areas where you can direct your mentoring.

Deeper Dive

English, M. C., & Kitsantas, A. (2013). Supporting student self-regulated learning in problem and project-based learning. *Interdisciplinary journal of problem-based learning, 7*(2), 6.

Hung, C. M., Hwang, G. J., & Huang, I. (2012). A Project-based Digital Storytelling Approach for Improving Students' Learning Motivation, Problem-Solving Competence and Learning Achievement. *Educational Technology & Society, 15*(4), 368-379.

Zimmerman, B. J. (2008). Investigating self-regulation and motivation: Historical background, methodological developments, and future prospects. *American Educational Research Journal, 45*(1), 166-183.

Project-based Learning

Lam, S. F., Cheng, R. W. Y., & Ma, W. Y. (2009). Teacher and student intrinsic motivation in project-based learning. *Instructional Science, 37*(6), 565-578.

Blumenfeld, P. C., Soloway, E., Marx, R. W., Krajcik, J. S., Guzdial, M., & Palincsar, A. (1991). Motivating project-based learning: Sustaining the doing, supporting the learning. Educational psychologist, 26(3-4), 369-398.

Jonassen, D. H. (1999). Designing constructivist learning environments. *Instructional design theories and models: A new paradigm of instructional theory, 2*, 215-239.

Ward, S., & Chapman, C. (2003). Transforming project risk management into project uncertainty management. *International journal of project management, 21*(2), 97-105.

CHAPTER 2

Know How You Mentor

Chapter Goal: This chapter is intended to inspire readers to become more aware of their own mentoring style and to define characteristics of a mentor that occur during a PjBL pipeline.

To develop a mentoring practice

You need to increase awareness of your own mentoring practices

So you can understand when, where, and how mentoring interactions will occur during a PjBL pipeline.

> *I remember my first mentor. I walked down a strange basement hallway at York University just north of Toronto and saw a sign on the door that read something like "want to go beyond classical or jazz piano playing and learn how to play whatever you want?". OK that's how I remember it, but it was likely not so cheeky. My mentor was though. I knocked on the door and after I inquired a bit more about the course, I was invited to come to the first class before I made up my mind. By that time, I had had my first piano lesson with a classical master I can no longer remember and I was thoroughly disappointed. Not for me, at all. I was done with Mozart. So, at my first Piano Improvisation class, everyone went round the room telling the rest of the class what brought them here, and I remember saying something like "Well, everything is improvised right? So even me being here is. Even me finding*

P. Parra Pennefather, *Mentoring Digital Media Projects*, https://doi.org/10.1007/978-1-4842-8798-9_2

out about this class by taking the wrong turn down this dismal hallway to this class." Chasey Cobolt—as we ended up calling our mentor one time—without missing a cue responded quickly, "You memorized that didn't you?"

Who was your first mentor?

In Chapter 1, you learned a little bit about the territory of PjBL in post-secondary including some of the ways students learn and the multiple types of roles you'll have to play. All those roles are bridged by the mentor, acting as a kind of ringmaster who presents content, listens to how students react, and responds accordingly. Just like in the workplace, there's not a lot of time to develop a systematic approach to how you mentor in post-secondary. This is partly because mentors draw spontaneously from their own experience when it comes to supporting a mentee in solving a problem that helps them develop a digital prototype with others. We all have our way of mentoring based on our professional experience managing, supervising, and guiding ourselves and others, all along different project pipelines with their own contextual demands. It's important then to decipher your own approach to mentoring by thinking about previous occasions where it emerged from your interactions in professional settings.

Mentoring Is

As you consider when and where you've mentored, you will likely come to a place of needing to define what you believe mentoring to be. It's not exactly teaching even though teaching might be one activity a mentor undertakes. In scholarly circles over the years, attempts have been made to go beyond a standard and simple dictionary definition. Scholars write about the subject of mentoring and try to break it down. They try and find the component parts that define it. This is helpful in that it helps us use more than one word to define what it is that we do when we mentor.

Figure 2-1 maps out some of the words that come to mind when thinking about the act of mentoring.

Figure 2-1. *Different words to describe mentoring from the literature and professional experience*

To Do: Mentoring Is

What's your definition? Use the visual model in Figure 2-2 or something similar and capture ideas that come to mind if someone were to ask you, "What do you mean by mentoring?"

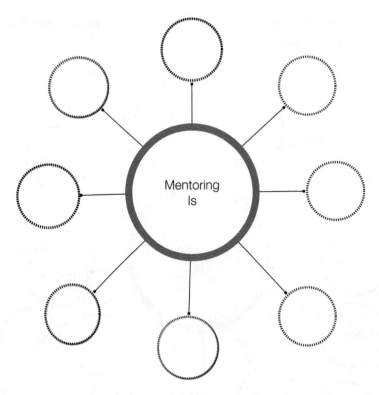

Figure 2-2. *A visual model to define what mentoring means to you*

Much of the literature on mentoring talks about the action of
mentoring as more of an approach to guiding others toward teaching
themselves, pointing them to what they might need to learn, supporting
their efforts at become self-reliant. You're not exactly a coach on the side
either although many of the characteristics of coaches and mentors might
be similar. Coaches can be more empathetic, whereas mentors might
be less. Both can also drive you hard to do what it takes to succeed. A
relationship with a mentor can last well beyond the time you are teaching
someone in a four-year undergraduate degree. Mentors seem to be more
concerned though about the learning that needs to take place and are
there to facilitate you in becoming more aware of how you learn. The
mentoring strategies that come later in the book are based on research

undertaken with mentors from the digital media industry. These mentors rely on a body of knowledge gained from real-life experiences in the workplace. That know-how is an essential part of who they are, and when shared with learners in an educational environment, it is an invaluable resource that can support students in enacting what they learn from direct experience that is as close as possible to the real thing.

Let the Mentor Be Summoned

At times mentoring can feel like juggling several simultaneous responses, personas, approaches, and responsibilities at the same time. It is difficult to predict what aspect of your mentor will come up when. What is somewhat predictable is anticipating the types of actions that a mentor will engage in because of responding to the environmental demands of a PjBL course. Mentors bridge the gap between acquiring knowledge and applying it. They guide individual and team learning. They identify the kinds of things students need to know in real-world settings and determine how to activate them throughout the PjBL pipeline. They manage learners to handle the prototyping process. They understand the types of personalities or personas that will work with the types of learners they encounter.

Mentors Bridge the Gap Between Acquiring Knowledge and Applying It

Distinguishing between teaching and mentoring within PjBL environments that are focused on developing emerging technology projects is a good way to understand how you will design your interactions. Whereas teaching involves directing learners to tools, approaches, strategies, methods, and use cases all to do with team-based project development, mentoring comes into play when learners apply what you have taught them to co-creating projects. Mentoring is activated when learners need to:

- Understand that constructing prototypes iteratively is a strategy to move beyond a conceptual understanding of a problem

- Associate the act of co-constructing prototypes as their combined efforts of attempting to solve a human problem

- Experience those inherent imperfections, flaws, and obstacle that form part of the process of creation itself

- Realize that another method of solving human problems is to prototype solutions in shorter time cycles instead of proposing a single solution over a longer period

- Manage their time and resources if they are to develop agency in solving problems on their own

- Learn to manage how much they can individually contribute over a specified period and become more efficient with how they use their time in the process

- Communicate persistently to ensure that all individuals are directing their aligned activities toward the completion of tasks that contribute to the features of an ever-improving prototype

- Become comfortable with the unexpected and adapt to changes to their intended vision and goals

- Resolve that the final features of their developed prototype can seldom be predicted and accurately scoped

- Affirm that unknown solutions that emerge through the act of co-creating prototypes will occur

- Integrate client needs and their shifting opinions on a project direction since they are part of a design process that is inherently unknown

Figure 2-3. *Attempts to solve a problem through prototyping in PjBL allow the actual problem to emerge*

To Do: Bridging Knowledge to Action

There are many other components of a production pipeline that team members need to know that will only be useful when applied to a project. Identify those components that you believe you will have to bridge through mentoring in its application on a project.

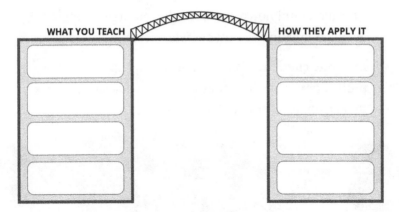

Figure 2-4. *Brainstorm what learners need to know and how they will apply it on a production pipeline*

Mentors Guide Individual and Team Learning in PjBL

Defining the learning that occurs within a project-based course through comparison of say lecture-based learning is often explained by what it is not. It's not exactly a course where students just build something even though they are constantly engaging with the co-construction process. It's not a lecture-based or theoretical course where students learn about principles of how to work together in an Agile environment to make emerging technologies.

In PjBL environments, learners engage in the "doing of it." It is not completely devoid of theory or criticality as might be misconstrued. Learners persistently engage in conducting research to understand what other projects might have been made that are similar. They also interrogate what they are making weekly to ensure that it solves a human problem. Learners providing feedback to one another can lead to the crucial learning outcome of creating self-regulatory teams. By interrogating their own design work, students understand that while their efforts may have resulted in a satisfactory result, there will always be room for improvement. Finally, they regularly test their prototypes and give each other feedback cyclically to improve the human experience of what they are creating.

One of the other challenges of PjBL being recognized in academic environments is partly because the focus of how people learn in project courses goes back and forth between the individual and the group. This presents a problem with many learning theories that primarily focus on understanding how individuals learn. Most theories of how scholars think we learn have informed how a course is designed. That has led to designs of learning that gravitate to what is easiest to manage, individual assessment. PjBL environments that demand collaborative activities challenge the dominance of individual assessment and attempt to balance this with assessing how individuals learn together. This is an important point to remember and will surface persistently in the remaining chapters. Mentoring supports individuals and teams simultaneously and will at times need to be focused on navigating learners to spend as much energy to improve their collaboration with each other.

Mentors Guide Prototyping in PjBL Courses

Learners in a project-based learning environment are tasked to build their knowledge and knowing through the rapid prototyping of a solution to a design problem in iterative cycles. The concept of rapid prototyping comes from software development and has become a design methodology, where a version of an idea is created through a specific medium, tested, and can lead to further versions that are more developed, may involve a different medium, and provide increased interactivity.

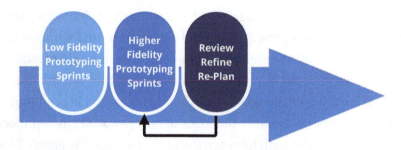

Figure 2-5. *Iterative cycles of rapid prototyping*

The design of a PjBL course, especially with projects focused on technologies that don't yet exist, follows similar cycles and patterns of evolution. Like the iterative process in project-based development, a rapid prototyping learning design involves developing a prototype that is tested on learners (users) whose capacity to understand content (the prototype) provides immediate feedback to the instructor (tester) who then makes changes in-the-moment and in-between classes. This shows us that adjustments to the design of learning are informed by the students who meet that design of learning.

A reflective practice will benefit instructors in a PjBL course combined with a capacity to be persistently observant to what is required and what might need to shift based on learner responses to the content, and questions they might have that reveal potential gaps that need to be filled. While the learner and the designer/teacher/mentor may have different learning experiences, they share one thing in common—they are both engaged in the act of problem-solving. While the learner is focused on solving the design problem as it relates to developing a digital artifact for a project, the designer/teacher/mentor is focused on responding to the process that each learner is applying to identify and solve problems, capturing interactions that they have with the learners, analyzing the situation, documenting it, revising their next interaction to plan the next prototype (class).

Mentors Translate Knowledge and Know-How into Authentic Tasks and Activities

PjBL environments provide learners with authentic tasks and learning outcomes that can be transferable to communities of practice they wish to transition into. One requirement for teaching and mentoring in this environment is to identify the kinds of things a person needs to know in real-world settings and determine how to integrate those into the design of a PjBL course. You already identified what types of components of a production pipeline learners would benefit from knowing and how you might bridge this knowledge in a PjBL environment. Now let's get more specific.

To Do: Begin to Plot Your Know-How and Knowledge

Using the visual model in Figure 2-6, differentiate between the things learners need to know and knowledge that would benefit them prior to entering your workplace environment.

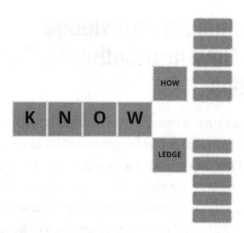

Figure 2-6. *Differentiate between what you know vs. what you know how to do*

After an initial brainstorm, it will benefit you to dive in more deeply, reflecting on the knowledge and know-how you may take for granted. These may seem obvious given your expertise, so it is important to unpack your assumptions of what learners should know and then plot activities that will support them in gaining both knowledge and know-how. To do so, do the following steps.

Step 1: Identify What Recruits May Need to Have Knowledge of

Identifying the knowledge recruits need to have may come down to the role they are applying for, and the accompanying skills required. There may be some knowledge though that would benefit them coming into your organization that they may likely not have. Think of when you or someone newer to the company came in to work and would have benefited from say being able to read an Excel sheet and contribute to one remotely. That may implicate a particular advanced level of knowledge with Excel that may even involve formulas to speed up workflow. What does advanced knowledge of Photoshop mean, or Unity? It might be important to think of specific workflows that colleagues in your organization take part in to better understand the knowledge base that is required. What are the important things to know and what are nice-to-haves?

Step 2: Identifying Experience in Production or Know-How

Know-how is commonly developed through experience. What you'll likely find is that many learners in a PjBL course have very little experience co-constructing a digital prototype, let alone any project. Assume that a student will come to the table with a strong desire to experience with little know-how, and therefore they will need to gain know-how through different defined workflows. Identifying some of those workflows may be a good way to start to think of how they fit within a PjBL pipeline. For example, what is the workflow required to create a physical prototype? What about a 3D asset? Go farther if animation is something you want learners to gain experience with. What is required to understand the workflow of animating a 3D character for a VR environment?

Step 3: Ask How They Might Come to Learn This Knowledge and Know-How

Mapping out the different ways that students will come to acquire knowledge and practice workflows that lead to know-how may seem a little daunting. What you will eventually undertake in subsequent chapters is to break down a typical workflow and then figure out how you are going to teach it, then have learners practice it. For example, what would be involved in teaching and mentoring learners how to work with separating an image from its background and then using that image as part of the user interface design for a medical application on a digital prototyping application like POP (prototyping on paper)?

Step 4: Use These to Create Activities That You'll Include in the PjBL Course You Eventually Design

Keep in mind that many prototypes learners engage in creating won't be constructed alone. They will each contribute to a collaborative process, and they will benefit from an assortment of activities you design that get them to practice making prototypes together. What do they need to learn to do so? This might also implicate collaborative values, drawing up Rules of Play and figuring out some way to manage their projects through Agile. They'll need to learn all those processes and then practice applying them through developing prototypes and then reflecting on the process.

Mentors Understand Their Different Personalities and Respond to Those of Their Mentees

Who you are as mentor will propel you to use one or more different types of mentoring strategies and influence how you mentor. The Mentor Persona map is inspired by a type of psychographic profiling common to human-centered design processes. Often with mentoring, there is not one but multiple personality traits or characteristics that mentees bring out in mentors. Those characteristics are often activated as a response to the mentee's persona, the situation, and the intervention that is called for. Figure 2-7 shows you a few that have manifested when facilitating PjBL environments in graduate and undergraduate environments.

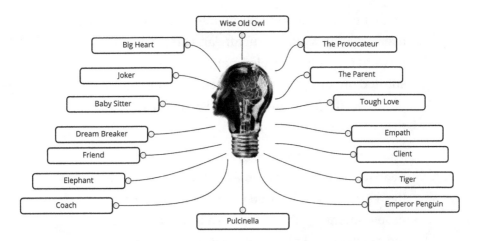

Figure 2-7. *Different types of mentor personas that surface when mentoring learners*

- The Wise Old Owl is crisp, precise, and to the point in providing feedback. When asked for an answer to a question, often the Wise Old Owl does not provide a direct answer, but a question.

- Big Heart is loving and affirming, always approaching learners with the intention of empowering them, feeling empathy for the challenges they face, and affirming their work.

- The Provocateur teases and at times picks on a mentee but always with the best intention in mind to point them to habits they are engaged in that will slow down the co-creative process.

- The Joker looks for opportunities to break the ice and take the seriousness out of things to laugh.

- The Parent may sometimes manifest and does so when a team requires more structure and discipline to move forward on project development. They are not mean-spirited but direct with what needs to happen, and often specific assignments are given to the team that they need to account for.

- The Babysitter is the type of mentor who feels they need to spend a lot of time with the team because the team may not be used to working on an Agile development pipeline. There is a balance of course as too much of the babysitter can lead a mentor to solve problems for a team that should really work toward self-agency.

- Tough Love persona is summoned to set things right when mentees start to stray from their own defined Rules of Play. That persona may come to the table with targeted interventions that they think will help the team. Be aware of this personality trait as it might sometimes come across too strongly or be used inappropriately. This personality is balanced with affirming students at the same time.

- Dream Breakers crush the blue-sky ideas when it comes to moving into production and they also help keep the team on scope. They don't need to "kill babies" as the expression goes. A simple reality check and explaining to learners why their fantastic idea may be out of scope and lead to disappointment is all that is needed.

- The Empath is that part of the mentor that affirms whatever emotional roller coasters might be happening with individuals or the team and then shifts their focus to demonstrating virtuosity and excellence. Be aware of your own boundaries in this case as you also need to ensure all students have the same opportunities and no one student is given too much latitude.

- The Friend is that rare quality that develops an amicable relationship with the team but is always cautious of keeping a strict professional boundary. Being present for the team when needed and sympathetic to their levels of stress that might come out of developing out of the unknown is sometimes comforting.

- The mentor as Client is tough, wants what they want, and you better impress them with your ideas and work ethic. At times teams need to respond to tough questions that the mentor surfaces, in essence acting as a surrogate of the client. Being clear that that's the role you are playing is helpful for students who can be let in on the joke.

- The Elephant is the mentor who removes obstacles acting in the best interests of the team and the success of the project. Their actions may not even be known to the team, as they respond to team obstacles as fast as they can to keep the momentum of the project going.

- The Tiger is the protector of the team when external forces attempt to bring harm, doubt, or trouble to any team member. Again, this is a personality trait that needs to be balanced as students will also learn a lot from standing up for their work and creating their own professional boundaries.

- The Coach hypes the team, gets them excited, and keeps them in the game, head high and ready to roll with the punches, a constant inspiration and relentless positive force. At times the coach may need to be summoned if a prototype gets torn apart by another team, or if any member of a team takes a critique about the project, personally.

- Emperor Penguin can to some extent and at times to the detriment of the team overprotect the team's feelings from being hurt, especially from outside critique. The intent is well meaning but needs to be monitored. Remind yourself of the learning outcomes and that student efforts may sometimes lead to productive failure is helpful in tempering the perfectionist.

- Pulcinella is a commedia character who plays dumb even though they are not, by walking through team offers, prototypes, and ideas to their at times flawed and humorous conclusion. Students tend to respond well to this personality trait, particularly when you take on the role of the user who happens to not know anything about technology.

To Do: Mentor Personas

After reviewing the visual model, which ones resonate with you? What types of personas are missing that you may actively embody in certain situations or have experienced before in others?

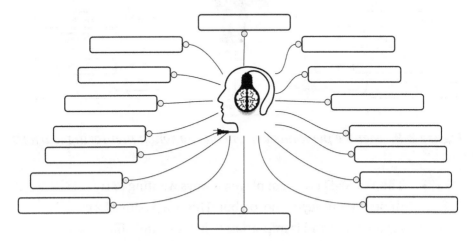

Figure 2-8. *A visual model to brainstorm the personas that surface when you mentor others*

Mentee Personas

It goes without saying that mentor personas are also provoked by mentee personality traits. The visual model in Figure 2-9 identifies many of the characteristics of mentee personas that you might encounter in learners, to varying degree.

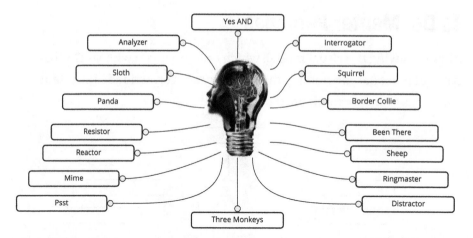

Figure 2-9. *Mentee personas you encounter when mentoring learners*

- The Yes AND is a team player, always wanting to try things before saying no, or, but. This is a positive force for the team and is important to nurture and affirm as that kind of approach can spread to other learners.

- The Analyzer likes to take things in and mull things over and in this process is usually silent but not absent. Analyzers are essential to a team makeup and often catch details that others miss. They can also empower other team members to increase their discernment.

- The Interrogator is that part of a mentee who constantly questions the validity of every single idea that is presented, which is usually a good thing but at times can slow the team down. The intent of the interrogator is what can be affirmed. In addition, that part of the personality needs to also be tempered with positive affirmations of what they are commenting on or critiquing, as it will build more trust in other learners and encourage them to make offers rather than holding back on them.

- The Sloth is a type of character who just moves slow on everything, often needing a lot of time to digest. They tend to take their time and slow teams down. That said, like the analyzer, they can also be highly detail oriented and that detail is important to the team. Individual goal-setting to rapidly prototype tends to balance this personality trait out.

- Squirrels are caffeine-fueled critters whose attention span is short but they can flit back and forth quickly between conversations, ideas, and activities. This capacity makes them ideal to lead rapid prototyping initiatives but a balance of taking time out should also be encouraged as they can quickly lose focus on the team and project needs quickly.

- Pandas are kind of clumsy and oafish and often respond to what the team needs, never really knowing what they are doing outside of their own work. That personality trait lives in each learner, and multiple daily status updates and other communication tools are helpful to support their capacity to be communicative.

- Border Collie's are astute listeners and make for good PM's nipping at everyone's heels to keep the team on track and are excellent at following the lead. Where they need support is in finding that fine balance between knowing when the team needs support managing time and knowing when they are micromanaging.

- Resistors resist and do so well. Even when you think everyone's on the same page, some type of response from the resistor will come out, at times in the form of a comment rather than a disagreement. Resistors can be placed in leadership positions at times to put them in a position of responsibility, but never at the expense of team mutiny.

- The Been There mentees always seem to come from a place of knowing, as if they have lived countless lives and lived all the experiences of every single member of a production team as they already know. These types of personality traits need to be challenged to take on something outside their comfort zone and even better if it's something that requires taking up a new skill.

- Reactors seem calm on the outside but have the tendency to explode under pressure and often can be seen taking a time-out. They have likely not had a lot of experience working with others or perhaps they don't really want to work with others. They may require time with you in a one-on-one situation to talk things through and possibly increase their tolerance for others.

- Sheep are not always easy to locate. They don't even need to say things like "I agree," as they just follow and enjoy being told what to do as they haven't really thought about it. When this personality trait overrides others, it is important to let them know that you see them, affirm their work, and challenge them to be more vocal in class.

- Mimes while similar to Sheep are generally the quiet ones; however, in secret and off the stage of a meeting, they will unleash their masterful vocabulary and will likely talk code. Like sheep, encourage mimes to speak as being vocal about their work, thoughts, and opinions will prepare them for doing so in work environments, which they will inevitably have to do.

- Ringmasters keep it all together and at times even question why they are there. They do need to be there because without a producer there is nothing to produce. They are good vision keepers and understand big picture. While they tend to shy away from leading, they might show potential and need some tips to do so.

- Pssts are the distractors who don't really know what's going on, so they ask someone else and then distract them and all of this because they are afraid to ask what they don't know most likely to not feel stupid. They may need more time to digest and will often understand if you say something in more than just one way.

- Distractors are a bit different than Pssts in that they really like to shine in the room whether showing off a new pair of shoes or the latest meme. Distractors are key to building team culture. They are not the best for keeping focus but can really support a team externally. When they are present, they are highly responsive and listen well.

- The Three Monkeys are the types of learners that don't really want to get involved in any of the politic and internal struggles of team members. They prefer to avoid working to resolve what is not their problem and do the work they are paid to do. In learning environments, this is the type of personality that will not say a word about how the team dynamic is going unless asked. Anticipate having to ask as teams often conceal any negativity as they believe their grades will be affected by this.

To Do: Mentee Personas

Map your own mentee personality traits as it is helpful to plan different strategic approaches when you see similar traits showing up as you start mentoring learners. Bear in mind that some learners may demonstrate aspects of one or another based on the situation and in particular the person they are directly interacting with.

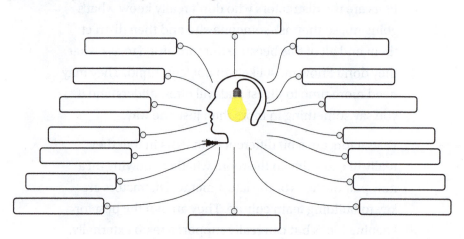

Figure 2-10. *Identify the types of mentee personas that you have encountered*

Chapter Summary

Sharing what you know in college or university settings will inevitably lead you to mentor and cultivate a teaching practice. To start that journey, in the next chapter you will benefit from understanding how, what, and when to teach the knowledge you have gained on previous production pipelines. This includes the tools you've used to keep teams aligned and the project moving forward.

This chapter:

- Suggested that you define what mentoring means to you as mentors bridge different types of roles you will enact when you facilitate a PjBL course.

- Proposed that you identify what learners need to learn on a production pipeline and how you would bridge that knowledge to its application through mentoring.

- Revealed different actionables to guide individuals and team, break down what can be learned through knowledge vs. practice, and translate these into activities learners can engage in.

- Highlighted the importance of mentoring the iterative process of prototyping.

- Proposed different types of mentor and learner personalities.

Tools and Suggested Processes

- Identify qualities and characteristics of what mentoring is to you.

- Brainstorm the knowledge and know-how that would benefit new recruits transitioning into your company.

- Mentor and Mentee Persona Visual model.

Deeper Dive

Dart, P., Johnston, L., & Schmidt, C. (1996, July). Enhancing project-based learning: Variations on mentoring. In *Proceedings of 1996 Australian Software Engineering Conference* (pp. 112-117). IEEE.

Ehrich, L. C., Hansford, B., & Tennent, L. (2004). Formal mentoring programs in education and other professions: A review of the literature. *Educational administration quarterly, 40*(4), 518-540.

Cranwell-Ward, J., Bossons, P., & Gover, S. (2004). What is Mentoring?. In *Mentoring* (pp. 26-44). Palgrave Macmillan, London.

Fagerholm, F., Guinea, A. S., Münch, J., & Borenstein, J. (2014, September). The role of mentoring and project characteristics for onboarding in open source software projects. In *Proceedings of the 8th ACM/IEEE international symposium on empirical software engineering and measurement* (pp. 1-10).

Pennefather, P. E. M. (2016). *Mentoring strategies in a project-based learning environment: A focus on self-regulation* (Doctoral dissertation, Education: Faculty of Education).

Zachary, L. J., & Fain, L. Z. (2022). The mentor's guide: Facilitating effective learning relationships. John Wiley & Sons.

CHAPTER 3

Know Your Various Roles: Designing Teaching and Mentoring Interventions

Chapter Goal: To better support you in assessing what students will require when working on projects together, this chapter will highlight your intersecting roles as mentor, designer, and teacher. The various roles you play on a PjBL pipeline will increase understanding of what teaching interventions will benefit learners the most as they dive into collaborative project-based work. Finally, deepening your understanding of what you know and don't know in terms of an emerging technology development pipeline will support you in planning ahead to design your course.

To guide students toward successful learning outcomes

You need to discern between what students need to know and the know-how they need to experience through practice

P. Parra Pennefather, *Mentoring Digital Media Projects*,
https://doi.org/10.1007/978-1-4842-8798-9_3

So you can design teaching and mentoring interventions throughout a project-based pipeline.

> *I walked away from the performance a wreck. It was a moment in time that I couldn't take back. My mentor in a firm but gentle voice said, "Don't worry no one would even know there was a mistake made. But remember both roles are just as important at the piano. You have to follow and anticipate what the player's going to do ahead of them doing it." Then the grin, "Of course, not too far ahead." He was reflecting on his just completed performance of John Cage's Three Dances, a challenging new music work that he was performing at Roy Thomson Hall in Toronto. I was flattered and incredibly nervous when he asked if I'd turn pages for him. I said yes and was more nervous than any concert I had ever played. Pages were turning incredibly fast and I had to follow and turn pages either when the player nodded or when I felt it was time. I was sweating more than the pianist. We now approached a complicated passage where the time signature changed about four times and I was keeping up. I was flying. I was doing this. First time. Woohoo. The music was exhilarating and the energy of the player fantastic. Then I listened in too closely and got lost. Oh no. Thank god he nodded though and so I flipped the page with renewed confidence that I had gotten back on track. No sooner had I flipped the page, then the pianist threw his hand up and flipped it back one. I had skipped a page and from that moment on vowed never to turn pages again.*

In Chapter 2, you were encouraged to begin to define what mentoring is, and start to break down your own mentoring process, even going as far as understanding that different types of mentor personalities in you can be activated by different types of mentees that you encounter. You learned that mentors can also be ringmasters bridging the student experience with knowledge and know-how.

You were also tasked to answer the question, "What would new
recruits need to learn and have experience of working on real-world
development pipeline?" You were encouraged to begin differentiating
between knowledge and know-how and to begin breaking down what
workflows might be taught in a PjBL course that you design. In doing so,
you will likely have identified what you know and what you don't know.
You may need to reflect further on how you learned what you know. Was
everything taught to you directly? How much of what you know did you
pick up from others? How might you design a project course to teach
others what you know? What will the balance be between teaching what
you know and mentoring students as they practice workflows? Conversely,
what workflows are unfamiliar or unknown? What is the balance between
what you know and what you don't know when it comes to emerging tech
development pipelines? How will you teach learners what you do not
yet know?

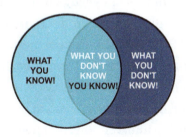

Figure 3-1. *Venn diagram visualizes what you know, don't know,
and what you don't know you know*

A Trio of Intersecting Roles

Whether a question that comes up about teaching a PjBL course is
about what you know or what you don't know, they will activate a trio of
intersecting roles: designer, teacher, and mentor. In PjBL environments,
these can be difficult to separate and that ability to move between roles is

highly dependent on your in-the-moment assessment of what you think
will most benefit learners. That could include knowledge areas you are
familiar with in addition to those you know less about.

For example, you could design activities that you will teach navigating
students to apply components of Agile that you speak to and provide use
cases for, and then mentor students as they apply that to a project. As you
observe how they apply what you've taught, you will likely notice gaps or
obstacles the students encounter that will inspire you to design learning or
mentoring interventions. Some of those obstacles you may also have not
yet encountered in your own production experience. Designing a teaching
or mentoring intervention in this case does not necessarily mean that you
have to be the one to deepen understanding of Agile. You could find other
resources and/or colleagues to visit your class and help both you and
learners increase knowledge. As the ringmaster of your own PjBL course,
you are not expected to know everything about every role on a production
pipeline, but it is important to acknowledge where those gaps are so you
can best support learners through the production process.

There is a back and forth between each of these three roles with the
mentor being the ringmaster that tends to observe, respond, and make
assessments in-the-moment. As you make assessments based on learner
actions in practice, rapid decisions may need to be made regarding
teaching and/or mentoring interventions that need to either be designed
soon or implemented right there and then. At times you will also need to
understand if the intervention that one team needs will benefit the other
teams in the PjBL course.

Because you can expect to move back and forth between teaching
and mentoring, it is helpful to design interventions that you can prepare
ahead of time and call upon as needed. Preparing as many possible mini-
or micro-teaching sessions for a team or entire class ahead of time will
benefit you as you move through a project course, particularly when time
becomes limited.

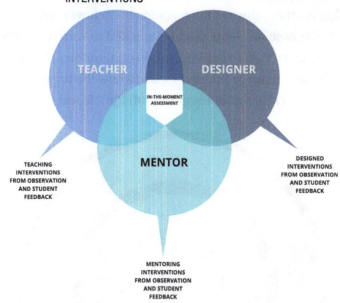

Figure 3-2. *Three intersecting roles when facilitating PjBL*
environments

Break Down Knowledge Areas Useful
to Emerging Tech Production

To move more seamlessly between mentoring and teaching, it is helpful to
break down all your knowledge and know-how in relation to an emerging
technology development pipeline that would be useful for students to
learn. You started to do so in the previous chapter. Bear in mind that you
will never be able to teach everything, so aligning what you teach with
your learning outcomes is important, in addition to leaving learners with
enough knowledge and know-how to continue their own learning journey
after they move on from your course. In addition to this, you will benefit
from using a bullseye visual model to prioritize those teachings that most
align with your learning outcomes. For example, in Figure 3-2, teaching
students about pipeline, prototyping techniques, and how to improve

collaboration is more priority than teaching them how to use Photoshop. In this particular case, students can be navigated toward resources online where they can learn how to use Photoshop on their own. Understanding how to collaborate, manage prototypes, and know the big picture of a production process also resonates more with PjBL learning outcomes.

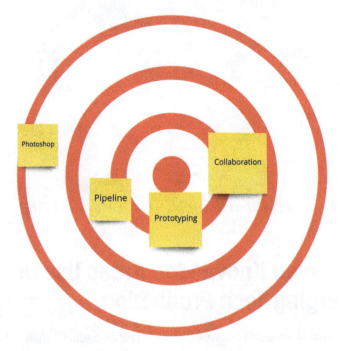

Figure 3-3. Prioritizing what needs to be learned in a PjBL course

To Do: Map What You Know

Looking at another example, the knowledge that learners enact on a typical production pipeline could be in the application of Agile as a project management methodology.

After you've prioritized what you think learners need to know, use Figure 3-4 to break down larger knowledge areas into some of the components that make it work. In the example of Agile, you could further break it down to include Scrum, Scrum Board, Backlog, Sprints, Retrospectives, etc. Take the time to rate your knowledge and know-how of Agile on a scale of 1–5. A rating of 1 means that you have recently learned how Agile works but do not necessarily have the experience applying it. A rating of 5 means that you've managed a variety of different Agile teams for several years. Reflect on why you rate yourself at a particular level. Recall that it is one thing to know about Agile and the working parts of it, and another to have a lot of experience or know-how on different kinds of Agile development pipelines. It will be useful to be honest with your own level of knowledge and know-how, as your understanding of Agile in practice will impact how well you can support learners overcome some of the hurdles when it comes to applying Agile processes to cyclic Sprints. You can use Figure 3-4 to brainstorm or draw your own.

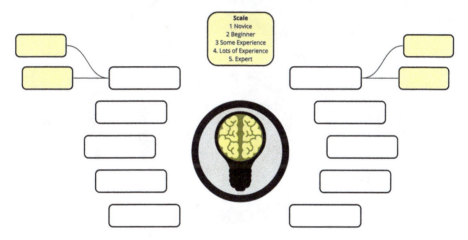

Figure 3-4. *Use this template to brainstorm and list what you know and rate it on a scale of 1–5*

Take note of low self-ratings and any knowledge gaps (example coding) as these reflections will inform you of how you will proceed when integrating features like Agile into your overall design of learning.

Teach Learners to Develop Skills and Capacities Outside Your Expertise

Repeat the use of the bullseye visual model to map knowledge areas and experience you do not have. In Figure 3-5, for example, you may not know anything about Agile but know that it is a priority when it comes to developing emerging technology. Keep in mind that you do not necessarily need to be 100% correct plotting what you don't know. It's best to uncover your own knowledge and experience gaps and then understand how to create interventions should you decide they need to be a part of your learning design.

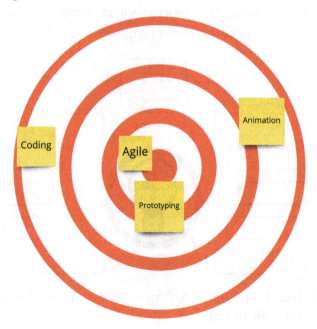

Figure 3-5. *Prioritizing what you don't know but feel it is important to know*

When it comes to the design of your course, you will eventually need to figure out how students will learn what you do not have expertise in.

This does not mean that you must immediately pick up coding or become a 3D artist or expert on Agile. However, it does help to know how the roles of programmer, 3D artist, and project manager contribute to and interact with an emerging technology pipeline. It is also beneficial to be able to know the latest tools that professionals are using in practice to advance those skills.

This is because students will need to eventually complete tasks they take responsibility for while simultaneously learning how to complete them. Part of your task as mentor is to guide learners to research and teach themselves what is needed to complete those tasks vs. teaching them how to complete every task on every project. What they may not know how to do is where to begin, so it is important to become familiar with the various workflows and experts that you can navigate them to. In the process, expect them to struggle a little with understanding the depth of knowledge they will require to be able to achieve project tasks. You may be able to bring in expertise in specific knowledge areas to lessen their worries and concerns. In preparation for doing so, you can also teach students the types of communicative and research skills that will help guide them toward asking the types of questions to ask an expert, whose answers will help regulate the knowledge required for students to complete tasks.

One gap could be in a knowledge area such as programming. You may understand how coders interact and relate to others in a specific pipeline, but you may not necessarily know how to code. It will benefit you to understand some of the resources you can point learners to who want to develop that skill during your course. It will also be useful to guide learners to experts that you may know who would support and possibly co-mentor a student in your course.

Chapter Summary

As you move into the next chapter, you will benefit from a better understanding of your own mentoring patterns when guiding others. Comparing the way knowledge is shared in workplace vs. learning environments provides valuable insights and will help you improve the overall design of learning.

This chapter

- Suggested that you map what you know and what you don't know so that you can move forward designing instruction for a PjBL course with more confidence.

- Underlined that there will be differences between what students need to learn to succeed within a PjBL environment as compared to in the workplace.

- Recommended that you identify what you cannot teach so you can plan ahead as to the resources and support you will need to secure to facilitate an emerging technology development pipeline in post-secondary.

Tools and Suggested Processes

- Intersecting roles when you instruct teams. Bullseye map as a prioritization tool.

- Mind mapping what you know and rating that knowledge on a scale.

- Mapping what you don't know but feel is important.

Deep Dive

Grant, A. (2021). Think again: The power of knowing what you don't know. Penguin.

Condliffe, B. (2017). Project-Based Learning: A Literature Review. Working Paper. MDRC.

Slough, S. W., & Milam, J. O. (2013). Theoretical framework for the design of STEM project-based learning. In STEM project-based learning (pp. 15-27).

CHAPTER 4

Know the Patterns of Mentoring and Teaching Interactions

Chapter Goal: This chapter will compare teaching and mentoring on PjBL pipelines with those you might find in real-world production pipelines. It will also reveal some of the patterns of learning that students will participate in.

To understand the roles that mentoring and teaching play in a PjBL pipeline

You need to compare mentoring and teaching interactions in workplace and learning environments

So you can Identify the patterns which will inform your design.

A man went into a shop and asked the shopkeeper,

"Do you have leather?"

"Yes," said the shopkeeper.

"Nails?" "Yes."

© Patrick Parra Pennefather 2022
P. Parra Pennefather, *Mentoring Digital Media Projects*,
https://doi.org/10.1007/978-1-4842-8798-9_4

"Thread?" "Yes."

"Needle?" "Yes"

"Then why don't you make yourself a pair of boots?"

(Adapted Sufi tale)

The Interplay Between Skills and Know-How

Pretend for a moment that you are guiding learners who have many of the available tools but just don't know how to access them to manage what they need to learn to co-construct projects together. It's not that they lack intelligence. They just might not be familiar with working in this way, nor do they understand that they have the capacity to 'make their own shoes'.

Students who enroll in a PjBL course will likely come from a variety of disciplines and will need to contribute to projects that are interdisciplinary in nature. This means that the requirements of a typical emerging technology project involve skills and know-how that come from different disciplines like programming, design, art, and management. Unless you have a team of teachers that cover all the bases, you'll realize quickly that you can't teach everything. Yet, you can mentor learners to teach themselves what they need to contribute to a project. Like the shopkeeper, they need little reminders that the entire team and, in some cases, the entire class have unique skills that can all be leveraged toward contributing to the projects in front of them.

Managing what you teach and mentor is similar in workplace environments. You don't stop a typical workflow at 2 o'clock and announce to the team that you will now lecture about optimizing art to reduce file size to make a VR experience more streamlined and to not overtax the graphics processor. In the workplace, learning is centered around mentoring individuals who are required to complete tasks that others are dependent on, communicate persistently, and improve how they collaborate. You mentor them to uncover what they need to learn to perform a specific task and remind them of the resources available to them.

Knowledge and Knowing in PjBL

In contrast to the type of PjBL environment this book describes, in many post-secondary institutions, teaching, and more specifically teaching through lecture, tends to be the dominant learning interaction. Learners are used to the lecturer as the gatekeeper to the knowledge they need to learn for that knowledge area. The unspoken contract goes like this. The sage on the stage stands and delivers and students are expected to pay attention, take notes to help them remember key points, absorb it all in, and then apply the knowledge they memorized during a test or exam. Other types of designs of learning have tried to break this pattern by providing social learning activities where students unpack a topic or solve a problem in pairs and share back to the group. Quizzes, tests, exams, and memorization of text or formulas form a large part of the summative teaching process. Teaching and mentoring in a project course are a persistent challenge for instructors used to teaching like that sage on the stage and students used to taking in knowledge in a passive way. There are no mathematical formulas to apply to a problem to solve and you can't learn Agile by simply memorizing all of its component parts.

What PjBL can do when designed effectively is break a passive pattern of teaching and learning. That change involves actively engaging students in every part of the learning process through activities that task them with building the knowledge and knowing they need while undertaking the development of project-based work. This new pattern of learning results in new interaction patterns that bridge what students learn with how they apply it. Be aware that some students will resist breaking those patterns of teaching and learning, because collaborative project-based work creates different types of demands on them that they are not used to. The key requirement, which some learners resist, is that of taking control of their own learning process and managing it.

As discussed in previous chapters, within PjBL environments, on any given day, teaching and mentoring are in a constant tug-of-war state. Your mentor as ringmaster decides on the type of intervention based on how students are responding to the content, to you, and to one another. Project-based work provokes a continuous conversation between instructors and learners.

Do the students on a team need more knowledge through a microlesson in the moment to proceed? Would all learners in the course benefit from the same lesson that can occur in the next class? Do students need mentoring in the moment?

For example, while students need to acquire necessary knowledge about an Agile project development pipeline, mentoring is what glues this knowledge together through the action of doing. This is because students gain experience or know-how as they co-construct projects together.

Identifying Patterns of Teaching and Mentoring

As an instructor, it is challenging at times to know what intervention is required when. But there is some hope. There do exist some interaction patterns where students might benefit from a combination of teaching and mentoring. Comparing patterns of teaching and mentoring that occur in the workplace in contrast to those that occur in learning environments can help clarify their differences. Knowing where you might expect them to occur in PjBL environments will support you as you think about how you will design your learning ecosystem.

Patterns of Teaching and Mentoring in the Workplace

Identifying and describing the differences between mentoring and teaching interactions in the workplace will provide learners with a better understanding for some of the activities that are essential to emerging tech development, but that they will likely not experience in a PjBL course. The point of learning what is needed in the workplace has more to do with contributing to the efficient and on-time delivery of a product, whereas in learning environments, it is more about learning different competencies through the creation of an incomplete deliverable.

Mentoring practices in workplace environments are similar in learning environments, whether formal or informal. Both can occur in an ad hoc way. In a company, mentors typically present themselves as coaches or fellow workers in more senior positions at the beginning of a development cycle. The amount of time they've been in a company may also inform the knowledge and experience they draw from. So might the amount of experience they've had in the same industry or similar position within any industry. In the workplace, mentors can act as provocateur to support the development of both individual and team heuristics, or how people solve problems. They also extend friendship and many times a mentee becomes an understudy to a position they eventually want to have, or at least one they think they want to have. In some companies, mentor matching forms part of the team culture, but these are not always mandatory relationships to develop.

Formal teaching in the workplace, while rarer, can take the form of

- Workshops that occur outside work hours. These tend to be optional for workers.

- Mandatory workshops focused on change management, leadership, culture-building and equity, diversity, and inclusion.

- In-house training on specific processes, software, and targeted roles especially if a role has a well-established history in a company.

That said, there is much ad hoc learning that occurs in the workplace whether it is to do with understanding how to improve performance on a team, time management, task completion, communication, or skill improvement. The reasons for learning in the workplace are certainly different. Knowledge acquisition in the workplace may be just as "messy" or "undirected" but may also be less formal in terms of when and how it occurs. The quality of work is assessed but by different standards and there is not often time taken for individuals to ask why it is they are engaged in what they are doing. The stakes are higher to learn what is necessary in order to ensure a product ships and deadlines are met. In the workplace, the goal of the mentor may be to ensure that team members have the support in place to learn what they need to succeed at delivering tasks the rest of the team is dependent on. Another goal may be to ensure that mentees transition into a team and company culture and have some support in solving their own problems if those problems exceed their competencies or level of skill. Mentoring activities in the workplace compliment work schedules, without taxing a team member too much so they can learn company software and pipeline, maximize production, perform consistently, and deliver on time.

Mentors support the improvement of learner contributions and relationships on self-governing teams and often reflect the cultural norms of the community of practice that mentors come from. Take time to identify the different ways in which your own work environment has affected you, how it might have created certain biases in your work ethic, communication patterns, etc. Often, when industry mentors work with learners, they are surprised by a lack of motivation, effort, curiosity, and commitment. How can you support learner buy-in to learning in a different way and transforming into a self-directed team member? In the workplace, very few have that responsibility, and a top-down approach tends to inform behavioral changes that are not helpful for teams.

In an educational environment, learners can better prepare for a workforce by also becoming aware of their own biases they may bring to project work and in addition to some of the behavioral patterns that are triggered when working with others. It is useful to articulate the biases you also may have. Here are some questions to ask yourself when it comes to understanding what patterns you come to the classroom with:

- What are some of the communication patterns that have come to be expected in your work environment?

- When a team member speaks, how have you and your team been conditioned to listen and respond?

- How are ideas that come from team members handled?

- When mistakes happen, what is the resolution process to avoid it from recurring, or is there a process?

- What are the power dynamics on the team and whose voices tend to be the loudest in the room?

Deepening your understanding of what you come to a classroom with will provide you insights on the types of behavioral patterns that may also manifest between students when they engage in creating together. Students may not be used to collaborating with others and have uncommunicated expectations of each other leading to all types of conflict. Some students will be uncomfortable with understanding that what they create by the end of the course will be unknown until at least the middle of the semester. Other students will be used to being assessed summatively through tests or exams.

Patterns of Teaching and Mentoring in Learning Environments

Teaching and mentoring in a PjBL learning environment require preplanning as synchronous moments with learners may be only possible once or twice a week. This is due to the amount of time that is expected from students and the credit they are receiving for their participation in the course. On the low end is a project course that is 3 credits and on the higher end 12 credits. The more the credit hours, the higher the amount of weekly interaction points will be expected from a mentor. Regardless of how much time students spend on a project, mentoring is anticipated, expected, and essential toward the success of the student, the project, and the course itself.

In project-based learning environments, the central goal of the mentor is to ensure that students learn how to produce with others through the act of creation. For would-be mentors, it is useful to identify and distinguish between interactions that require teaching vs. those better defined by mentoring. This will help you to design learning interactions that are more intentional in their anticipated learning outcomes.

Your approach to mentoring will be modified based on whom you mentor, how much real-world experience they might have, how quickly they respond to your prompts, the degree of time you spend with learners, outgoing vs. more reserved personalities, and the number of interactions you have with them weekly. It is important to consider the scope of a project and the time expected of each learner on it. The more time you have, the more you will be able to provide individual mentorship. The larger the scope of a project, the more likely learners may require mentoring. At times anticipate that not all learners will readily approach you for mentorship. This is in part informed by their personalities, but it may also be that they are not used to approaching instructors in this capacity. In fact, they may not even know what question to ask.

Although mentoring often manifests as the primary interaction between a mentor and a learner, mentors still must engage in planned and ad hoc teaching activities. Project-based learning environments demand a balance between teaching and mentoring. This can be observed at all stages of the design. While you can't teach people how to solve problems for themselves, you can teach them to identify how they solve problems and build into the curriculum design that they must solve problems that come up.

The Impact of a Weekly Schedule on Teaching and Mentoring

Typically, weekly class time is set aside for synchronous interactions with an entire group and tends to revolve around a predesigned teaching objective. Classes are generally structured with a short lecture around specific topics related to digital media production, followed by group activities that relate to the development of a digital media project. In this way, teaching and mentoring merge as learners engage in activities that tend to link directly to professional practice; the results of which are reviewed and assessed according to the practices of the professional community in which the mentor/teacher belongs. Mentoring sessions tend to be structured within time limits that work for the mentor as well as the mentee. Mentoring during synchronous and prescheduled class times tends to be directed toward the group vs. one team or individual. However, as the learning pipeline develops so do the projects, resulting in a decrease in teaching and an increase in mentoring.

In PjBL we can at least rely on weekly patterns of interaction since classes tend to occur once a week with work in between. Figure 4-1 depicts a cyclic pattern of teaching and mentoring during a typical project-based class. Both types of learning interactions coexist and interventions are dependent on in-the-moment reflection by the mentor. For example, you might teach about different types of prototypes and then create small groups of 4 for students to practice paper prototyping. Targeted questions about what the prototype is depicting, what a more fleshed-out prototype could look like, and the problem students think that the prototype solved can all be facilitated. Based on student responses and understanding of a paper prototype, you can choose if they are ready to continue with a new lesson, repeat and improve based on feedback, develop a physical prototype, etc.

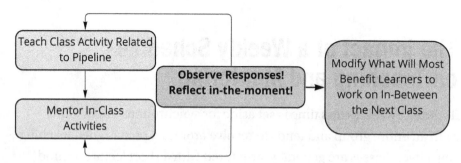

Figure 4-1. *Modifying what you teach, and mentor based on learner responses*

Projects in a learning environment allow both teaching and mentoring to coexist in as-close-as-possible simulation of a real-world digital project workplace pipeline. The key difference is that a project in a learning environment does not need to be part of the critical path that it would on a real-world project. This affordance allows you to freeze the project development process at any point you need in order to reflect on how the learners are doing. In that pivotal moment, you decide what's necessary and design micro-teaching interventions, redesign what might need to be taught next, and in many cases rescope the balance between teaching new tools and mentoring teams who are applying existing tools. An example might be to freeze the development process if students on a team are presenting low-fidelity prototypes that don't address the core problem to be solved. This may be an opportunity to take a few steps back and ask the rest of the class what problem they think the team's project is solving. The interruption is an important learning pattern in that it allows students the space to correct and reorient themselves toward a more directed path.

Signs to Watch for That Inform an Intervention

There may be a wide variety of learner responses to an activity, content, other learners, or you that signal a need to freeze the development process and shift gears toward a targeted intervention.

- Questions or confusion that students might have about the prototyping process itself. They may also require a use case before proceeding. Some students are more comfortable than others working with general instructions.

- The application of tools that learners have been asked to use to solve problems. A perfect example is the use of prioritization as a strategic tool (see Appendix 1) to get to the core problem to solve. A lack of familiarity with using the tool will slow down or even stop a team's process, so it is important to integrate more complex tools within class time in addition to taking the time to observe how more complicated tools are applied.

- Confusion with terms such as scope, pipeline, features, and how they apply to project development.

- Reflection and/or reaction on the current "playable" state of the project. Timeboxing feedback is an important strategy when facilitating feedback sessions. If, however, student responses to another team's prototype are plagued by confusion, then it's a good

sign that the team may need a meeting to recalibrate
and be clear on what they are creating.

- Team communication and collaborative issues that
  may have surfaced as the team approaches solving
  problems together. These will tend to require time away
  from the rest of the class and can be scheduled during
  your office hours.

Design Features That Will Require Teaching and Mentoring

When you will teach and when you will mentor cannot always be
predicted, but you still must design a course and communicate that course
outline to students prior to starting. As you begin to think about that
design, it is beneficial to identify specific PjBL features that will require
teaching, what will demand more mentoring, and what will require both.
Figure 4-2 shows features that will require mentoring and teaching.

Figure 4-2. *Some PjBL design features that will require a combination of teaching and mentoring*

Project Charter

An agreement document that may have preset sections that outlines what a team will deliver, who the team is composed of, and the roles they will take on. Teaching the template is the easy part. Learners will require mentoring in order to describe the project they are undertaking and the problem it solves.

Design

Every aspect of the design process will require a little bit of teaching and a lot of mentoring. Learners will benefit from learning a number of human-centered design processes including visual models to help them problematize. They will then need persistent feedback from their iterative attempts to solve a problem through increasing levels of a prototype's complexity.

Kickoff

During kickoff, learners practice their communication skills with their client partners and with each other. They are not used to meeting with a client and proposing their ideas, responding to client challenges, and being able to better understand what is being asked of them. These sessions typically require mentoring as learners need to go through it in order to understand afterward what worked and what could be improved upon in the next meeting.

Ideation

During ideation, students will apply many of the tools that you propose to help them brainstorm ideas, prioritize them, and move them toward defining a project whose interactive features will address and solve a problem that was presented to them in a Project Brief.

Project Management

Learners will likely not be used to managing projects together and will not come to a team with a defined process. They are more used to creating projects on their own or with one or two other people, but that doesn't mean they've adopted principles of iterative design. Teaching components of Agile (see Chapter 7) and mentoring its application throughout a project will benefit students.

Rules of Play

Rules that govern the behaviors that teams tolerate and those they do not are an essential part of a process that summarizes the core values that a team defines. Rules of play for team-based work are essential for learners to determine and will likely need mentoring in order to fully articulate some that they come up with. An example is that many teams highlight respect as both a Core Value and a Rule of Play. This makes sense. Important, though, is in understanding that the word respect and its accompanying actions mean different things to different people. Breaking down one word Values or Rules of Play is a strategy to encourage learners to articulate thoughts that they likely have but have not been encouraged to communicate.

Team Collaboration

Collaboration and its principles can be taught but can only be understood when applied in action. Many of the challenges that occur on PjBL pipelines are a direct result of inconsistent or nonexistent communication patterns. A focus on how teams communicate, including the practices of listening and responding to others, affirming each other, and talking things out even when difficult, will benefit from your mentoring.

Heuristics

Heuristics in this case refers to the process by which each individual solves problems. Heuristics tend to fall into patterns for many people and their way of solving a problem may not always align with another person's methods. Teaching about heuristics and drawing individual attention to articulating how they solve problems will improve the overall way that teams solve problems. A focus on problem-solving with teams will likely take some of your mentoring time.

Client Meetings

When the opportunity presents itself, facilitating client meetings is one of the best ways for students to learn about how they present themselves, their ideas, and how they treat one another and a client under a variety of pressures. It's important to observe small details in client meetings that you can address with the team after the meeting. These mentored post-client meeting reflections go a long way in increasing student awareness of how they interact and can lead to many individual and team breakthroughs.

Mitigating Student Jitters

Be aware that what students must learn and then apply in a PjBL course might at first appear overwhelming to them, especially if they lack the technical skills to co-create technology. It is important to assure them that co-constructing a project together is not only possible, but that all the tools they will need to do so are within reach for them to learn. This is because of the increase in maker tools that have been developed and the abundance of free tutorials on how to use software that is specific to developing emerging technologies. It is helpful to create a resource list that can be shared with learners and to have them also add ones that they uncover throughout the course.

One of the goals of facilitating a PjBL course focused on emerging technology development is to encourage innovation. That spirit of innovation can lead to creative experiences that learners may not have the opportunity to experience in any other course. Transforming interactive patterns within a PjBL environment also means providing learners with the opportunity to

- Create versions of the same project in cycles persistently improving and increasing in complexity over time.

- Spend time creating something that doesn't end up solving the problem like they thought it would.

- Become more skillful in scoping what it will take and how long it will take to develop something brand new.

- Learn new skills without the same pressures they might have in workplace environments.

Chapter Summary

This chapter and the ones before have prepared you to brainstorm what needs to be taught and what needs to be mentored in PjBL environments.

As you move forward into the next chapter and those that follow, core features of PjBL will be uncovered that you can begin to associate with both types of learning interactions.

This chapter

- Discussed teaching and mentoring patterns in the workplace that might inform your design as you begin to understand where and when teaching and mentoring interactions will occur during a PjBL course.

- Suggested modifying what you teach and mentor in the moment based on learner responses to content.

- Introduced signs to watch for when mentoring and/or teaching interventions will be required.

- Highlighted design features that will require a combination of teaching and mentoring.

Tools and Suggested Processes

- Visual map of features to anticipate designing teaching and mentoring interventions for.

- Approaches to mitigate learner uncertainty and fear when tasked to co-construct projects.

Deep Dive

Mergendoller, J. R., & Thomas, J. W. (2005). Managing project-based learning: Principles from the field.

CHAPTER 5

Know What Needs to Be Taught and Mentored in PjBL

Chapter Goal: In previous chapters, you've identified what you believe a person needs to know (knowledge) and how they can apply it in action (know-how) on a typical production pipeline. You looked at teaching and mentoring patterns in the workplace and how these could be applied to PjBL environments. Many of these interactions are mentoring ones, yet they need to also include teaching interactions. Now that you've brainstormed what you already know and identified gaps in your work, it is useful to get more specific as to some essential teachings and mentoring that students will benefit from in PjBL courses focused on emerging technology development. This will help you to better understand the kinds of learner interactions you will encounter over the course of a PjBL pipeline.

To specify what you will teach and mentor in a PjBL course

You need to understand all the teaching and mentoring elements and how they integrate

So you can more effectively understand the relationship between both in your design.

© Patrick Parra Pennefather 2022
P. Parra Pennefather, *Mentoring Digital Media Projects*,
https://doi.org/10.1007/978-1-4842-8798-9_5

Setting the Stage

In this chapter, what needs to be taught and mentored seem like two distinct activities when in reality, they are intertwined both feeding off each other. The visual models that represent what first appears to be a dizzying amount of knowledge and know-how that needs to be integrated in the overall design of a PjBL course draw upon aspects of teaching and mentoring. For example, you can teach all you want about how to solve problems and plan activities that bring more awareness to students about how they solve problems (heuristics) but they will need to be mentored to solve specific design problems that come up. In fact, they will need to iterate on identifying core problems that their projects will solve in the form of interactive prototypes. The action of solving problems in this case needs to be both taught and mentored. Consider the sections that follow as a starting point for that integration. When considering what needs to be taught, keep top of mind that the application of anything that you teach will then require mentoring.

What Needs to Be Taught in a PjBL Course

Figure 5-1 depicts what aspects of an emerging technology pipeline will need to be taught assuming most learners do not have experience with developing any technology. Some mention of mentoring will be made for each of the larger categories as well.

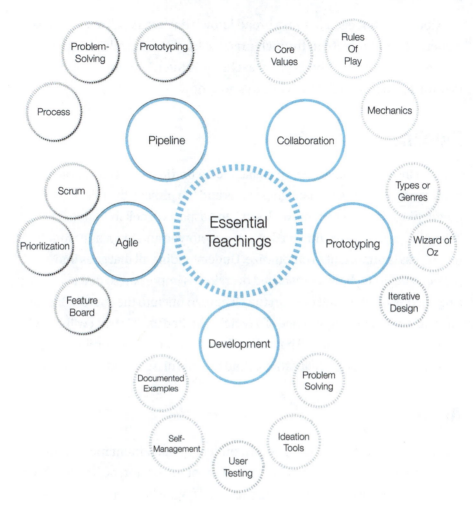

Figure 5-1. *What typically needs to be taught on a PjBL pipeline*

Teaching learners within project-based courses has multiple meanings. Teaching manifests as a combination of mini lectures that explain important parts of a production pipeline, giving tangible examples of what learners will need to take on informed by that pipeline, modelling and then facilitating short activities that support learners to be able to tackle different components of an emerging tech pipeline, and reinforcing different components of the pipeline by having students present assignments that they work on in-between classes.

Consider that each of these broad knowledge areas will also require students to embody them through practice for them to truly "stick." How successful students embody your teachings is interdependent on the mentoring you provide that leads to know-how.

Pipeline

Introducing what a pipeline is in digital media production, its component parts, the role of Agile in managing teams and the project, the role of prototyping, the idea of iterative design, and aspects of collaboration. The balance between taking time to develop a prototype and test it as a work in progress is important to emphasize. Understanding all that goes into a pipeline including how it's managed over time is important so that learners get a big picture of what kind of effort they'll have to put into the course. Breaking down and providing experience of a typical pipeline itself is what will allow learners to gain know-how. That will include how they start a project, tools to ideate, tools to manage their process, and the role of Agile and prototyping.

Agile

The language and intent of Agile as a project management methodology that supports the continuous improvement of the prototype, the team, and the individual can be taught. Components of Agile like Scrum, Sprints, Scrum Board, Backlog, visualizing work in progress with Kanban, are important to integrate into your teaching pipeline. Overall, it's important to emphasize that project creations are continuous works in progress with the goal to improve a set of features over time that the team decides will contribute to some type of minimum viable prototype. The other essential quality of Agile is to emphasize the need for persistent communication by all members of a team. This can be achieved by reinforcing weekly touch-points and using asynchronous and synchronous social work channels to remain in touch outside of the classroom. Finally, visualizing progress helps teams get an immediate sense as to where they are at. Maximizing the number of features helps teams avoid scope creep and allows bottlenecks to be exposed in terms of unforeseen tasks that may only emerge once work is undertaken.

Prototyping

Related to the strategy of iterative design is the foundational need to teach learners the purpose and importance of prototyping ideas that solve a human problem. Along with providing use cases and allowing time for students to create conceptual, paper, physical, and digital prototypes, it is important to integrate cyclic reviews. These reviews will require facilitation and allow space for you and other students to question the functionality of a prototype. The relationship between time and prototyping should be discussed along with the intent of a prototype that can be tested. The idea of scaling up a prototype over time needs to be practiced so learners understand how earlier efforts contribute to the development of features that come to define the final MVP, or minimal viable prototype, that they will deliver at the end of the course. Prior to scaling up though it is essential that prototypes address the problem to be solved. In some cases, this may not occur and that situation provides an excellent learning opportunity as students may need to abandon a prototype and create anew. That spirit of engaging in cyclic versions of low-fidelity prototypes is a fantastic way for students to understand their purpose. Prototypes are not intended to be the end result of student efforts. They are intended to best represent an interactive artifact whose basic components are intentionally designed to solve a human need or problem. Presenting prototypes cyclically allows learners to better understand the types of questions that will come up when users interact with them. These provocations challenge learners to get into a mindset of continuously improving what they have, building on its strengths, abandoning features that take away from the core experience, and always keeping the problem to solve top of mind.

Collaboration

One of the most challenging yet important areas to teach is collaboration. Every single individual on a team will have a different idea of what makes for good collaboration, so there needs to be some type of aligned understanding in order for everyone to become more aware as to what aspects of their behaviors and actions enact collaboration and which prevent it from being nurtured. This can in part be achieved in facilitating scaffolds that support a collaborative process by teaching learners essential tools and designing mini-activities that bring more awareness to how they collaborate. Breaking down what qualities of collaboration are important with the entire class allows you and the students to better understand divergent perceptions of collaboration. We can't just assume learners are innately prepared to work on emerging tech projects together when they likely have had very little experience working on projects with others at all. Activities to engage in are ones that draw awareness to how they listen, how they share and receive ideas, how they communicate, what they pay attention to, how important empathy is, setting up core team values and they can find alignment with, and more. Providing persistent opportunities for teams to share their collaborative experiences including successes and challenges also helps individuals feel that they are not the only ones doing the right thing, or the only ones, struggling.

Development

Throughout the pipeline, there will be different opportunities to teach related skills and competencies learners will need to fulfill a project. These include teaching them about different ways to solve problems and activities that bring awareness to how they problem-solve alone and together. Understanding their roles and the associated tasks they need to complete is also important, along with learning what they need to specifically learn to achieve those tasks. For some, this will be challenging.

It must be clear to them at the beginning of the semester, however, that they will need to manage their time learning new software or other skills to be able to complete tasks embedded within graded assignments. Again, when learners apply the knowledge of development, it will be important to address challenges as they emerge and offer support as often as is needed. That support may not take a lot of time. Learners at times simply need affirmations that they are on the right track because many will not really know if they are. A careful balance needs to be struck with letting students figure out problems on their own that you know will lead to failure, and supporting their efforts more intentionally when you notice the project is heading down an unsuccessful path. There is an overall misconception about the role of failure in the development process in PjBL. It's not like your intent is to necessarily set learners up to fail. Students will make mistakes in the design process because of not having the experience to consider all aspects of the user experience they are designing for. The important aspect is to catch early impulses that could lead to efforts being misdirected, or if you prefer, failure. These impulses can include the following:

- *A misunderstanding of the role of prototyping leading to first versions being of too high fidelity and resolution*: The fix here is to facilitate the team to take a step back if the representation has missed important aspects of the human experience or does not address the core problem to solve.

- *Communication challenges with each other*: An emphasis on persistent communication that all team members can agree on may be necessary to facilitate, including response time thru whatever communication media they are using.

- *Inability to go to too much depth on a personal or group activity*: Often times students come to a PjBL class with very little experience visualizing their reflections. When it comes to reflecting on the prototyping process, there is a tendency to summarize feelings, thoughts, or ideas into single words or a short series of words. Encourage learners to go deeper by simply asking them for more detail.

- *Creating something "cool" vs. something that solves the core problem or need*: Students may navigate their efforts toward building something that has plenty of fireworks but does not address the core problem they set out to solve. It is important here to acknowledge the beautiful display and also task them with taking a step back in terms of the fidelity of a prototype and return to the purpose of prototyping, which is to address and provide a solution for the core human problem or need.

What Needs to Be Mentored Throughout a PjBL Course

Figure 5-2 details the essential experiences that will require mentoring during the co-construction of an emerging technology project. Notice that the "ing" words show what needs to be mentored as active and in process. You will notice a crossover between what was highlighted in the "What Needs to be Taught" section that you read previously. You will notice specific tools that will need to be modelled first and then assigned to students to complete either individually or as a team. Each of the following ideas will be more detailed in the chapters to come.

Figure 5-2. What needs mentoring during a typical PjBL pipeline

Self-Regulating

Mentoring learners to self-regulate is one of the most reported outcomes of PjBL in the research literature. There are many attributes or characteristics of self-regulation including the capacity for students to manage their own learning, maintain the self-motivation and energy to do so, be able to set personal goals, manage their health throughout a production pipeline, manage peers, manage time and tasks, manage the relationship with the client, and persistently assess the performance and quality of work. Learner actions and performance do not necessarily need to be managed by you. They need to be mentored to manage themselves. In many situations, learners will come to you for the "right" solution, when they might propose better ones if you hold up a mirror. Although it may seem at times that it is easier to solve a problem for them, allowing learners the opportunity to take responsibility for solving their own problems teaches them to manage what they need to in order to contribute to a group task, assignment, or project. You can also draw attention to specific use cases of teams that may have solved similar problems, especially when those teams did so independently. Demonstrating related use cases or recounting stories of self-reliant teams will benefit learners.

Problem-Solving As a Team

While you may not need to solve problems for your team, it is beneficial to provide them feedback when they need it to better understand how they are solving the problem they currently have. Encouraging them is one part of the solution. The other is to provide them some scaffolding when required and to ask questions about what they are doing. The process of scaffolding involves teaching learners the knowledge that they need to provide them a strong foundation. Prototyping can be seen as a form of scaffolding. Through various types of prototyping, students learn the value of iterative design, testing features, and making changes to their prototypes based on feedback. Prototyping can also help learners identify a problem to solve they might not have initially recognized. For example, students in the past have often revealed paper prototypes that demonstrate some type of interaction that will occur in VR. What they haven't shown visually is a 360 environment and where a person starts on their journey. They might just have the expectation that a user will know where to look or even what to do first. The prototype reveals that the team has not taken into account the user's journey. Several layers of problem-solving are encountered. The first is the realization that the prototype has revealed a new human-centered problem to solve. The lack of defining what a user needs to do first in VR will prevent them from having any other need that the VR experience is supposed to fulfill.

Learning by Doing

Learners are not really equipped to co-construct prototypes that lead to some type of emerging technology when they first arrive in your class. They have likely been conditioned to rote learning models before their encounter with you. Some may have become familiar with social constructivist learning environments where they at least have learned the value of social learning activities and have developed some communication skills. Asking learners to perform and learn while doing may seem very unfamiliar to many of them. Supporting learners in persistently engaging in the act of doing is what you will likely mentor the most on a typical project. That will include actively applying what they learn to the development or co-creation of prototypes. Students will get used to the cycle of learning how to use a human-centered design tool, like a persona visual model, creating one on their own, presenting and receiving feedback on it, and then revising and refining a version two of that tool. This cyclic process of creation followed by feedback allows them to embody the way of learning in the class. While many will be unfamiliar with it, it does not take a long time to get used to the rhythm of learning by doing.

Collaborating with Team Members

Learners have been mainly taught in environments that celebrate and assess the efforts of individual performance. While they might have been involved in small projects, assignments, or in-class activities that require collaboration, most likely a larger weight of their grade has not been assigned to a final project. Mentoring learners to collaborate requires you to balance your interactions with learners on a weekly basis. This will be dependent on how the team is applying the tools you taught them to remain aligned, communicative, and socially engaged with one another. You will find all kinds of responses to the challenge students face in collaborating with each other. Some will avoid wanting to have too many touchpoints with their team members. Others may have not had positive experiences with others and will end up doing their own project. Relying on the inherent components of an Agile pipeline will help students learn quickly that their work can be both independent and dependent on the work of others. Emphasizing their inter-connected early in the process will support them in these realizations.

Managing

Managing each other, the project, and a potential client are all important features of a PjBL course. Learners will likely have had very little experience with management tools like Agile. They will need to first learn all that is involved and then be mentored as they apply it to their own projects. Managing collaborative prototypes over time will be new and challenging, particularly the feature of cyclic design and continuous improvement. One of your tasks will be to help a learner understand the importance of managing themselves and not solely depending on a project manager to do so. This navigates learners toward taking on personal responsibility for their own work, resulting in increased self-reliance. Many learners will have a persistent challenge with timeboxing, so tasking learners to commit to estimating how long individual tasks will take allows them to understand the importance of improving task estimation and how proper estimation influences project scope.

Developing an Equitable, Diverse, and Inclusive Team Culture

There exists an abundance of tools that you can teach teams to develop a flat culture, where every voice counts and where every decision must be made democratically. Of utmost importance is to model this in the classroom by treating every voice in the room equally and navigating learners to share their intelligence. One of the things that will help you is to identify the tools and processes that you've engaged in within your workplace environment. If you have not, it is important to understand where you stand on the value of creating equitable, inclusive, and diverse teams. Students are smart and often they question the values they grew up with, comparing them with others and reevaluating both. Ask yourself what combination of teachings and mentoring might be effective at encouraging students to think about equity, diversity, and inclusion when they form teams, share opinions, allow others to speak before they do, etc. Once you are face to face with learners in your first class, it will benefit you enormously to open up a discussion on historical challenges with underrepresented voices in the field of technology and to also show use cases that champion EDI (equity, diversity, and inclusion). You may want to bring in a leader in the field to speak with students as well. One of the most effective set of tools to use when you first gather with learners is to facilitate two visual models: Core Values and Rules of Play. Each will allow students to voice their opinions on what the Core Values of the class itself should be and how these can inform Rules of Play. There are also a few important things to know when you facilitate a PjBL course in a post-secondary institution.

- Students will already be joining your course with a clear opinion and experience of power differentials that are embedded within every educational institution. This is because of the agreement a student makes with themselves when they decide to study in an accredited institution. Somebody must grade their effort in order to progress within a particular program they have chosen. Their perception of success in the course may differ from an instructor's perception of that effort so it's important to refer to a rubric that details how you arrived at their assessment.

- Students have different ways to communicate and at times one student may trigger another and may not even know it. A good example is the common mistake some learners make of referring to their target users as male. This will trigger those who do not identify as male and it is important to interrupt and task that student to reframe, simply because their perception of all users being male is likely incorrect.

- You need to prepare for the possibility that some team members may not deliver what they are assigned to. This will impact the team and what they have agreed upon to deliver. An unfortunate but at times necessary reason to reaffirm your grading rubric with students in this case may be called for.

- Other students will want to overly manage their teammates creating a tense situation of control and mistrust. This may provoke resistance, bias, and an overall discontent between students on a team.

- Some students may not be communicative in class for reasons you may not at first understand. These may have to do with power differentials, with negative experiences that have been imprinted in the past, cultural reasons, or shy and quiet personalities.

- Inevitably at different points in the pipeline and especially in the beginning six weeks, you will need to mentor learners to weigh equal importance on nurturing their own team culture as they will on the project co-construction itself.

In some cases, learners who don't feel like they belong, for whatever the reason, don't usually communicate this until the end of a semester. Depending on your own lived experience, background, and experience supervising diverse teams, you may miss some signs. It is important nevertheless to be on the lookout, and you may mitigate this for some students by setting a rule of play with the class at the beginning that whenever they feel like their voice is not being heard, they should talk with you one on one. It's important as well to invite students for midterm check-ins. These do not necessarily have to be about providing an assessment but can simply begin by asking a student how they are doing in the class and on their team. The more you are able to get a pulse as to how individuals are doing on their respective teams, the more you will be better able to design and implement activities that accurately deal with challenges of diversity, equity, and inclusion provoked by bias, misperception, misunderstanding, and ignorance.

Comparing Teaching and Mentoring Activities in PjBL

Knowing that teaching and mentoring will both play a large interconnected part of a PjBL pipeline, it's useful to compare when, where, and how they manifest during a course. This will come in handy when designing your interactions and determining the amount of time you will spend teaching and mentoring. Table 5-1 compares some of these differences.

Table 5-1. *Comparison of some of the differences between mentoring and teaching in formal learning environments like PjBL*

Mentoring	Teaching
Tends to be informal but can be scheduled.	Is more formal and schedule dependent although ad hoc interventions may occur.
Can happen anytime, just in time, or immediately following a teaching intervention.	Happens at scheduled times although ad hoc micro-teaching interventions can occur when an instructor notices a gap in learning or realizes that a subject may need to be taught again.
Dependent on the situation as expressed by learner offers or responses to provocations.	Situations are more designed although the reflection that follows may yield unexpected results.
Mainly focused on the individual or team during the class time or in-between classes.	Dominantly focused toward the entire class and sometimes teams either during a class or in-between classes.
Assessing how individuals, teams, or an entire class are doing is usually based on their response to activities, questioning, or responses a mentor makes to what learners present. This assessment can often result in a repeat of an activity, a variation of it, the presentation of a use case, or a brand new but related activity that might support their greater understanding of the material.	Assessment is formative with set milestones to grade learners on what you define in the grading rubric. In other words, specific participatory and assignment criteria that learners fulfill can be assessed in every class, and through each assignment that is graded. A final or summative grade must be given, however, as this is usually a requirement of most programs in post-secondary institutions.

(*continued*)

Table 5-1. (*continued*)

Mentoring	Teaching
Mentoring tends to occur a few times a week in-between classes and in class when necessary. Sometimes and with some individuals, mentoring might occur more frequently.	Scheduled teaching sessions tend to occur once a week, although you may point them to remote resources that describe a tool or process and lead to their fulfillment of an assignment.
Feedback as to how learners demonstrate their understanding of a tool or process can occur immediately. New feedback can also recur after you have thought more deeply and with more time about what a team presented or submitted.	Feedback tends to occur after a set period. That feedback can be weekly based on assignments that learners submit. Feedback in the form of a letter grade on course performance tends to occur at predefined milestones. Exceptions include spot quizzes to test where learners are at with understanding specific knowledge they learned previously.
Mentoring is not that familiar to learners. Grad students may refer to it as project supervision even though the role of a supervisor in most universities refers to some type of thesis a student undertakes.	Teaching interactions like lecturing are very familiar to learners. There will be some degree of difference between paired or group activities that an instructor facilitates.
The role of a mentor, while not defined, attempts to dissolve power and status differences between them and learners. This is not always successful, though, since a mentor still transforms into a teacher who provides a grade to a student at the end of the semester.	The role of a teacher in post-secondary institutions is usually of a higher status. The power dynamic tends to be assumed where the teacher has power over assessing how a student learns and, in the process, can influence their future status as a student.

Shift Between Mentoring and Teaching Interventions

It is increasingly clear that in PjBL environments you will need to summon your mentor and your teacher. This will be dependent on the situations in which you can expect your mentor to be more present at times, and at others you will need to identify what formal micro-teaching intervention will benefit individuals, teams, and the entire class. When teaching and mentoring in PjBL environments, it's difficult to predict how teaching or mentoring will be received by an individual, team, or the entire class. It's helpful to understand when you might freeze development to either teach or mentor. You may not have the time to intentionally construct a teaching intervention or model a particular tool or process. Other times if you do not possess the knowledge, you may need to point to a resource, or find the support for the mentee.

While mentoring tends to be directed toward individuals and teams, teaching is usually targeted toward the entire class. Yet, due to the unpredictability of the project's flow and how students are progressing with it by either applying or adapting the tools you taught previously, you may need to find micro-teaching moments in a team session. Table 5-2 offers a comparison of some situations that have come up and how they manifested as a combination of mentoring and/or a micro-teaching intervention. The table presents a handful of examples but more will likely emerge provoked from the unique needs that students may have.

Table 5-2. *Comparison of the difference between mentoring and teaching specific topics*

Mentoring	Micro-teaching moments
An individual or the team may approach you for advice on how they can improve their workflow. When solving the team problem through mentoring, most likely it will be in the form of advice, pointing to a resource or memorable stories.	In this case, you may need to dig deeper into what the problem is. This can be either mentored or the use of specific tools can be facilitated. You may ask them to repeat their Scrum from earlier in the day. From that, you may better understand what the obstacles are for the team. You may have to repeat and remodel the use of tools like prioritization using a bullseye, defining user stories, making commitments to time estimations, and encouraging teams to try timeboxing and minimizing distractions in their project time.
At times a team or learner will be confused as to how to perform a specific task related to their project. In this case, it will be beneficial to talk through what the task is and ask them to brainstorm a process.	The inability to understand where to start with animating a 3D character will require you to point the student to existing online resources that point to workflow. They may not have the vocabulary to understand how to search for the solution so much of what you teach will be related to defining terms to help them know where to go for help.

(*continued*)

Table 5-2. (*continued*)

Mentoring	Micro-teaching moments
Many learners are unable to manage tasks over time. This is because they lack the know-how to properly estimate, but it can also be caused by being unable to manage their project tasks in the course you teach with all of their other courses. In this way, they will benefit from timeboxing and practicing their improvement of task completion on a weekly basis.	Scrum board, Scrum, Agile, and the application of a project management tool like Trello all need to first be learned and modelled. Only afterward can students start to apply them in practice. Anticipate that they will get stuck and at times may require micro-teaching moments to remind them as to how to apply a tool to their project work.
Learners are not used to communicating work completed and work to be done. They are used to handing in assignments on deadlines so it will be necessary to speak to the timing of their task completion and also talk about dependencies and the necessity at times to complete tasks that they have way before the next class when they meet together again.	The use of a digital scrum board and/or a project management tool can be taught in addition to making sure students understand how the tasks they are taking on contribute to features that the rest of the team is also contributing to.

(*continued*)

Table 5-2. (*continued*)

Mentoring	Micro-teaching moments
Most learners are used to communicating obstacles or challenges but have not done so in a structured way with others on team-based projects. The form of Scrum is easy enough to memorize but student responses at times need to be elaborated upon as they might miss important details as to the work they are completing and how it involves other team members.	Scrum, Weeklies, and Status updates are all great structures to teach, and status updates in particular are necessary to repeat often so that students come to understand the importance of persistently communicating where they are at in the project pipeline.
Adapting mentoring to the variety of different approaches learners have when it comes to solving problems.	Problem identification, root cause visual models, and explaining heuristics.
How to show work in progress.	Prototyping (document, screen capture, digital platforms, paper, physical, Wizard of Oz, digital mockups, mood boards).
How to make offers to others and help others.	Facilitated feedback sessions, improved games like Yes AND.
How to manage what needs to be learned to deliver a task.	Self-management, library of resources, workflows and learning management tools.

Whereas in the workplace these situations tend to come out in an ad hoc way with specific contextual examples targeting individuals and usually in the flow of a project pipeline, in a teaching environment, each of these elements can be organized to be taught as modelled in-class activities that become assignments, in combination with individual, team, and class feedback and mentoring. These can better prepare learners for when they manifest working on real-world projects with others after they graduate.

Chapter Summary

There are many approaches to mentoring students to apply the skills and competencies they learn toward their undertaking of an emerging technology project together. Those strategies are unique to each person and will be important for you to define in the next chapter.

This chapter

- Highlighted the interconnection between teaching and mentoring, and how you'll draw on both.

- Introduced experiences that will need to be taught and mentored in PjBL.

- Compared teaching and mentor activities in project-based learning.

Tools and Suggested Processes

- Visual model demonstrating what is essential to teach and mentor in PjBL

- Table comparing mentoring and teaching in PjBL

- Table that compared use cases where a combination of mentoring and/or a micro-teaching intervention might be required

Deeper Dive

Grant, M. M. (2002). Getting a grip on project-based learning: Theory, cases and recommendations. *Meridian: A middle school computer technologies journal, 5*(1), 83.

Almulla, M. A. (2020). The effectiveness of the project-based learning (PBL) approach as a way to engage students in learning. *Sage Open, 10*(3), 2158244020938702.

CHAPTER 6

Know Your Mentoring Strategies

Chapter Goal: This chapter will present some mentoring strategies drawn from research to support the development and articulation of your own.

To think about the mentoring interactions you will have with learners

You need to analyze some mentoring strategies drawn from research

So you can leverage your own and make more intentional decisions as to how and when to use them when interacting with learners along a production pipeline.

Now that you've been presented with how mentoring and teaching intersect in project-based learning environments, this chapter will focus on uncovering mentoring strategies drawn from research, some of which you might relate to and use. This chapter is the largest in the book as it attempts to provide you with strategies that can be drawn from when mentoring learners.

© Patrick Parra Pennefather 2022
P. Parra Pennefather, *Mentoring Digital Media Projects*,
https://doi.org/10.1007/978-1-4842-8798-9_6

A Strategic Approach to Organizing Your Mentoring Strategies

There is no single approach to mentoring in PjBL environments since the composition of every digital media project is unique. If you have experience mentoring in a game studio, you may have found that every game pipeline is unique, along with the team of individuals that contribute, their varying levels of experience, and the type of knowledge and knowing that they need to "ramp" up. The strategies you will use are those methods you have more than likely become used to: the go-to approach, what is second nature. There is value in taking the time to become more aware of the strategies that you use to mentor and in what situations you used them. This way, you more intentionally draw from a strategy that you feel might work for the situation at hand.

An important and often overlooked strategy to consider relies on creating a contract, some type of written agreement where both parties agree on the scope, scale, and style of mentoring that will fulfill the course requirements and address more specific nuances in what the mentee would find useful. In post-secondary contexts, this typically does not happen. Students are used to being handed a course outline before the course starts where the content, rules of conduct, schedule, and assessment procedures are "understood." Mentor and mentee will benefit from developing a more intentional and carved-out mentoring agreement.

Mentoring Strategies Drawn from Research

The following typology was developed out of research conducted at the Master of Digital Media Program in Vancouver, Canada. Research was conducted with several mentors from the digital media industry representing the animation, games, and mobile development industries. The strategies outlined were used by the mentors on specific projects.

The typology is a useful reference point but by no means complete. This is because you may align with some strategies and not with others. Importantly, the strategies are meant to inspire you to brainstorm your own. For this, you can use a typical mind map or a similar visual model as the one in Figure 6-1.

Figure 6-1. *Mentoring strategies demonstrated in graduate PjBL courses*

Modelling

A common mentoring strategy drawn from research in PjBL environments is modelling. If you've ever shown someone how to do something by doing it, then you've modelled. For example, modelling lets mentors demonstrate how they might solve a design challenge that is specific to their own industry experience. The timing of a session where you might model is not usually planned and can be triggered by individual or group

109

interactions with the project or client. The process of modelling includes the demonstration of behaviors that are related to the community of practice a mentor belongs to and has the potential to accelerate learning when similar approaches come out of student efforts to solve problems together.

Examples of modelling include the following:

- Arriving on time for meetings and being present and undistracted. Modelling this behavior, while it may be second nature, is important for learners to experience. It demonstrates professionality and challenges learners to consider the value of being on time and being present and ready to listen, collaborate, and work.

- At times a mentor may need to facilitate something they notice has not been integrated into a team's project pipeline. This is common especially if learners have never experienced a collaborative project before. In some cases, it may be a visual model on a whiteboard to help learners outline the Rules of Play of the team. In other cases, it might be that they have not fully done the work on who the project is for. In many cases, a mentor will need to support learners in properly identifying a problem to solve.

- Modelling client reactions with a mock client meeting that the mentor goes over with mentees to practice.

There are different types of approaches to modelling:

- Chunking or breaking apart the steps needed to consider how to solve a complex problem at times using some type of template or visual model as a mnemonic device

- Starting the first step of a problem to solve and then eliciting what next steps learners can take based on what they've learned in class

- Walking through how to use a specific visual model as an example of how to solve a problem and then have learners do it in relation to their own project

In research conducted at the Master of Digital Media Program, a student was observed imitating their mentor's method of Socratic questioning when they were addressing another team member. The first student asked, "What would you have done different to come a little more prepared for the meeting?" The second student responds to the first continuing the flow of the conversation without the mentor interfering. "I would have met with all of you beforehand and asked what our team wanted out of the meeting."

To Do: Reflection on Modelling

What have you modelled that your team benefited from? Did you wish you had modelled a process or tool that you had not after reviewing a team's results?

Feedback

"I don't like you," a student could be heard saying from around the corner of a project room. "I don't like you either," replied another teammate. "Fine," said the third student. "Let's use another pronoun."

(overheard while walking past a project room)

Feedback is a natural process that is encountered in working and learning environments. At times, feedback can be misinterpreted. It can feel like being attacked even though that may not have been the intent of the feedback that was given. A whole range of feedback methods are employed informally and formally in the workplace when compared to designs of learning. The object of the feedback, how much is given and timing of the feedback and assessment that sometimes follows, however, is quite different.

Table 6-1. *Comparison of feedback in workplace and PjBL environments*

Workplace	Project-based learning environment
Focus of feedback is to improve performance related to execution of tasks associated with the role someone was hired for.	Focus of feedback is to improve learner understanding of the content of the course in addition to assessing how learners learn.
Stakes are higher as assessment informs livelihood, job security, and therefore life security.	Stakes are lower although for students, assessment also impacts career path and, in many cases, affects continued scholarships that diminish the cost of learning.
Performance reviews impact a person's future in that job and at times in the industry itself since communities of practice are often interconnected. A bad review leading to being fired will not do a person well.	Persistent reviews are meant to improve assessment and impact learning and can influence a learner's transition into a community of practice. A bad assessment usually results in a fail giving those who do, the option of repeating a course, or securing another arrangement with a professor.

(*continued*)

Table 6-1. (*continued*)

Workplace	Project-based learning environment
Goals to reach may be defined together with clear outcomes that affect a person's ability to perform well for the team. Some companies use goal-setting frameworks but not all.	Goals to reach may be defined but can be a bit fuzzy since an individual learner may not be in a defined role nor fully understand what they want to do. Important, though, is to get learners to do so. These can also allow them further agency within a predefined set of curricular goals. Most of the time, personal goals are in alignment but there are some exceptions, and these can and should be considered.
A team is not usually assessed however team performance being the sum of the individual parts that make it up is looked at as an indicator for the company itself and team makeup may change as a result. Underperforming teams will require intervention and the tendency is to either hire new team members, reset management, or shift high-performing individuals to underperforming teams.	Team assessment is crucial in supporting individuals to develop collaborative skills. Team makeup can also be assessed, and shifts may occur. Learners have more choice as to which team of individuals they want to collaborate with. Many students don't really care what team or project they are on. Certain individuals on teams will outperform others and care should be taken in affirming the individual as much as the team. Some learners will coast and let the higher performers carry the weight. It is crucial to identify them through specific individuated assignments and to review task responsibilities every Sprint.

(*continued*)

Table 6-1. (*continued*)

Workplace	Project-based learning environment
Peer feedback is informal unless facilitated. Some companies have formal processes in place. These are usually anonymous. Care is not always taken in the design of feedback systems where bias and unhealthy intentions (i.e., deliver more) can sometimes override the intent of continuous improvement.	Facilitated peer feedback is common and useful in learners affirming one another and also learning how to give and receive critique on work in progress.
Work is reviewed with high expectations based on company vision and reputation. In some exceptional cases, companies may support promotion for those employees who take training or upskilling offers.	Work is reviewed with the intent to improve upon it as there is no real expectation for a specific type of prototype at a defined level of fidelity. Learners typical ask for exemplars so they can better understand what constitutes an A over a C+. It is difficult to persistently gauge this accurately but important to design rubrics that reflect your review of work.

In project-based courses, regular feedback is a strategy to persistently ensure that learners understand how they are doing, because how they do eventually translates into a grade. In many cases, those grades come a bit too late for learners to make changes to patterns of learning, and as a result, learners tend to leave a course unsure of what they learned. As a result, many instructors across disciplines have introduced grading milestones to ensure that learners are provided with a sense of how they are doing so they can at least have a chance to improve.

In PjBL courses, the relationship between performance and assessment needs to be considered. While that will be more detailed in the last chapter, providing feedback along the way (formatively) especially when initiated after direct engagement with a learner's understanding and application of a tool or process is beneficial.

A feedback scenario might look like this in PjBL. A team has been taught specific human-centered design techniques and has completed assignments related to the project they are undertaking. All the assignments look good on paper. A persona map has identified key characteristics of their user. They have storyboarded a day in the life of their projected user which, while well executed and of surprisingly high fidelity, is still missing some steps.

So how do you assess that?

Maybe your first impulse is to grade the assignment as to how well it fulfilled the criteria. That's fine; however, oral feedback on the assignment is essential to walk through what might be missing in the user's experience. If done in class, then all learners will benefit from walking through a specific assignment and understanding what might be missing from it. Providing learners the opportunity to self-assess is an important process that can also reveal their own biases as compared to the rubric you've defined, and how excellent vs. mediocre deliverables are assessed from your industry standpoint. Assessing learners on how they assess themselves can also inform the grade you give them.

While specific situations like the scenarios outlined earlier influence the type of feedback that a mentor will provide, there are broader areas of feedback you can expect to give learners.

- Students need feedback on their overall approach to solving problems including the identification of a problem to solve.

- They also need support "scoping" a project, estimating the amount of anticipated work and time that it might take to realize their own or a client's vision over time.

- Mentors can test the learners' understanding of the "core idea" (the central idea that solved the design problem) of their project and provide feedback on how well they thought the learners understood what problem the project would solve.

- As detailed in the highlighted scenario, learners need persistent feedback on all the possible interaction points a potential user/customer/audience will have with the prototype they are designing. That feedback helps them improve all aspects of the user experience (UX).

- Strategically, mentors can also test learners with challenging questions to anticipate how their client might respond to their next round of ideas and prototypes.

- The concept of user testing can be more broadly applied to every artifact that learners present in front of you and the class. Feedback on more formal user-testing protocols is also important from the type of research they want to create, to how to deal with data, ethics, and how to improve a prototype based on user responses.

Feedback given to learners who are working on projects affords learners one of the defining features of self-regulatory behavior—a self-reflective feedback loop. That loop consists of a cyclic process in which students monitor the effectiveness of their learning methods or strategies and react to this feedback in a variety of ways, ranging from changes in self-perception to changes in behavior.

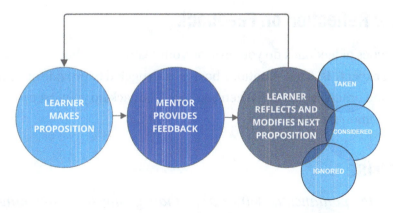

Figure 6-2. *The cycle of a learner making a proposition, receiving feedback, and making changes*

Learners need to hear the same feedback in a variety of contexts and from a variety of sources (not just the mentor) for them to assimilate the feedback as a lesson learned. To reinforce their feedback, mentors can bring in guests who will likely provide feedback that echoes their own. Having external client partners whether from industry or from teaching or research faculty at the university also provides another source of important feedback.

One of the advantages of having interactions with client partners is that it offers mentors another opportunity to provide feedback based on their behavior toward one another and the client during a meeting. Learners can receive direct feedback from clients based on the presentation of their ideas or pitches, and how they conduct communication remotely and in-person with them. Post-client meeting debriefs afford learners multiple opportunities to "get it right" even if it involves a repetition of the same feedback they might have received earlier, or by another stakeholder in the project.

Finally, it is important for learners to track and document what they learn from a feedback session and, specifically, how they will apply that feedback moving forward. This will accelerate their understanding of how they contribute to the overall project, and the design process.

To Do: Reflection on Feedback

What types of feedback do you provide your teams and what actionables do you expect? In what situations have you struggled to provide accurate, clear, and timely feedback? When you give feedback do you first try and find common ground?

Surprise

"I do spontaneous 360's rather than giving them anything ahead of time. Or even when they ask, 'So what's the purpose of this 360?.' I keep it very vague until I'm there, because I tend to prefer answers that haven't necessarily been rehearsed in their mind previously. I want to get their first impressions and then later on I can follow up and then they've had time to really think of stuff. I tend to believe that whatever comes out of their mouth first can be more along the truth. That's really what that person does. If I give them a lot of time to come up with an answer, there could be a lot of b.s."

(Mentor interview from conducted research)

As in the preceding case, at times mentors surprise learners for strategic reasons. Surprise questions, challenges, or facilitated activities test a learner's ability to articulate their own understanding of a project, and what their peers are contributing to the project in the moment without rehearsal. The strategy of surprise keeps learners "thinking on their feet" and provides them the practice of generating unrehearsed responses regarding their performance and the performance of their peers. By not always preparing learners for what is to come, mentors attempt to demonstrate that no matter how much preparation ahead of time, in real-world situations learners will likely have to contend with all manner of unexpected events.

For those learners who are used to adhering to a strict agenda in which an entire class agenda or in-between lab they plan with one another is outlined ahead of time, you may encounter some resistance. That's OK; at times, it is necessary to surprise learners and "catch them off-guard" and then ask them for a status update on the project or ask them what problem they think their project is solving, etc. This *spontaneous disorientation* is an expectation common to the communities of practice many learners will be entering and provides them with practice in articulating the current state of their projects along with problematizing certain design challenges they are currently engaged in. Balancing that disorientation is helpful as too much may lead to instability. Discussing the scenarios where this might manifest in the workplace is also good to share and may help learners understand the difference between working under pressure and knowing their own boundaries of what may provoke too much stress.

To Do: Reflection on Unplanned Feedback or Interventions

When have you had to provide unexpected feedback to or interventions with your team and why? Are there situations in which cyclic feedback sessions would resolve the need to provide ad hoc sessions? How were the responses to the feedback you provided? Was the feedback you provided helpful and when was it unhelpful?

Unplanned feedback is common across industries, particularly those developing any emerging technology, so it's important to gauge how that feedback is received and the results that occur from it. This may also inspire you to reflect on the healthy and perhaps not-so-healthy practices of your workplace.

Timing

Learners sometimes need a lot of attention, and at other times, it's best to let them work out a problem on their own. Problems tend to be related to their own capacity to complete tasks, a team alignment problem, challenges with understanding pipeline, or a lack of buy-in on the client-proposed project they are working on. Timing your mentoring will always be a challenge but each project and team has its flow that will help guide you as to when an individual or team needs more mentoring. There do exist some indicators in PjBL environments focused on developing emerging technology. These can help you predict when teams will need more support and when they might need less. Some of those include the following:

- The beginning three weeks of the course will be a time of orientation. Learners will be excited by all the new processes and tools they are learning but a lot of confusion may result because these may be unfamiliar, as will the methods in which they are learning them. Expect more time to be put in at the beginning of a PjBL course.

- Once teams are formed and get settled, there may be rumblings as to how their roles relate to the tasks they need to complete. Going over what those tasks will be over the course of a semester may prove helpful to them and reduce how much individual and team mentoring you will need to attend to.

- Teams that don't communicate how they are doing persistently or how their project is moving forward are both indicators that they have not assimilated the importance of persistently keeping you (and a potential client partner) up to date. You may notice and be able to tell in the moment if sufficient work is being done by a team when they present what they have achieved. Clients may also have a completely different communication pattern than what the team believes. This makes it important to facilitate a discussion on communication. At times teams will need to be guided as to where they are in the pipeline, what their priorities are, and what tasks they need to complete as next steps to move the state of the project forward.

- Individual team members may be provoking other team members to respond negatively. The persistent provocation may be coming from one or two team members, but the result is usually a dysfunctional team that underperforms. As an example, one or more students may be extremely negative regarding the project itself. They may feel like they were mismatched by being assigned to the project. They could be highly critical of the project or client itself. This might happen even though most of the team is content to work on the project as it is. In this case, you'll likely spend much more time with the team and in one-on-one sessions with the disruptive elements in addition to those who are unable to manage that behavior. While providing mentorship in this case, it's a bit different than in the workplace since the focus is on learning, not on performing their job. As you mentor each learner, bear in mind what they could learn from this situation. Focusing your efforts to guide learners to solving interpersonal problems by learning more about themselves, their boundaries, biases, their behaviors, and response patterns will provide them with a learning experience that will help them when they begin to transition into a community of practice.

- The final buildup of the course requires more attention to all teams ensuring they have what they need to successfully deliver their project on time. Of course, you and the team may also need to contend with unexpected obstacles that delay the deliverable date. Students being unwell may also influence the timing of a deliverable in addition to its scope. Presentations of final projects and preparation for documentation replace a typical exam as learners must present their project in a concise manner and they also need to articulate all aspects of their progress in written form. After the final class, there will still need to be team interactions to ensure learners are fulfilling all the requirements you set out for final documentation. You will also be in part responsible for supporting students to better understand and assess their own success on the project and how to gauge the success of their project itself in solving a human-centered design problem while satisfying a client. A final project Retrospective can be modeled using some type of feedback instrument (see Appendix 1: Retrospectives).

Be aware that work social channels integrated into a project course project while useful also means that careful boundaries of use may need to be adhered to within a team's agreed-upon working hours. As a mentor, you will provide much of your feedback and responses to learners in-between classes on social work channels. There are many protocols on remote communication you can follow and, importantly, be clear with learners at the beginning of the first class of your communication style on these channels, reminding them as well that their teams will need to create Rules of Play around communication and access hours. These are further affirmed with persistent check-ins as to how the team is managing those initial Rules of Play, and if they have been modified. Some teams pin up their Rules of Play if they work together in-person as this allows those rules to become an important centerpiece for their team activities. All that said, teams quickly forget some of the finer details of the Rules of Play they once deemed essential. Some team members have fantastic memories where others do not. It is important to address what the team will do when a Rule of Play is not adhered to or forgotten. Having some type of conflict resolution process in play may help students understand that identifying Rules of Play is not just an exercise that can be considered complete and left alone for the rest of a project cycle.

Finally, the timing of the mentoring immediately following a client meeting is a strategic way to capture reflection while it is still top of mind.

> The "important thing is catching how it went immediately after the moment because they're still doing a personal reflection... because they are really wondering how they did or whether or not something they did, didn't happen, or whether they should be cheering that their idea or their comment in the meeting was the one that won the day."
>
> *(Mentor interview from conducted research)*

Humor

> "Our supervisor's sense of humor really helped us in tense times when we were stressed out. I remember one time he came in halfway through a Sprint joking that the client had pivoted. We all looked shocked then he smiled and said, 'Oh I meant postponed. He wants to postpone the next meeting to a week from now.' I think we cheered because there was no way we were going to be ready in two days."
>
> *(Student interview from doctoral research)*

Humor is a great icebreaker with new teams and when applied to high-pressure situations can bring levity to what might otherwise be a stress-inducing moment. It's a way to level the playing field and remind students that they never need to take things so seriously as to have any work-related situation affect their learning or mental wellness. The use of humor is aligned with the intention to make the inherent challenges of solving ill-structured design problems a less frustrating experience. By moderating the complexity of certain design problems and their team's occasional inability to identify problems with humor, mentors give learners permission to see their contributions as part of a generative process where each moment of interaction is an opportunity for dialogue, exchange, and humor. Through humor, mentors allow learners to lessen self-judgment, and become increasingly unattached to their design and prototypes. That unattachment does not mean they should lower their personal investment in what they are co-constructing with others. It is a way to prepare learners for an industry that is constantly striving to make the output of all its humans, better, and the process of creation, more fun.

Humor allows fun, enjoyment, and laughter to be part of the process of learning, an idea that is not practiced widely enough. Recent studies in neuroscience point to the brain's release of dopamine provoked by laughter. Dopamine is a neurotransmitter that activates reward-motivated behavior and in the case of project-based learning can increase student buy-in to the project, team, and tasks at hand no matter how daunting they might first appear.

Humor in the form of ironic interplay with the students can also be intended to provoke learners to consider the full extent of their actions and their plans of action where you can play out their offers to an extreme. A note of caution however: be prepared to call out the kinds of humorous jabs, and ill-intentioned pokes that demean someone, that make someone feel "less than"; are racist; show bigotry; reveal sexism; are antagonistic, sardonic, and persistently cynical about a client or project; or are persistently self-deprecating. Humor can be targeted at situations but should not be targeted at people.

Socratic Questioning

"What is the secret to wisdom?", a traveler once asked a famous monk. When the monk did not reply, the traveler had an insight and walked away smiling.

—Anonymous

Figure 6-3. *The cycle of Socratic questioning consists of asking a question, waiting for a response, and then responding with a statement or another question*

While mentors let mentees follow their impulses even if it means going down a path that doesn't address a core problem to solve, they regularly prompt learners to respond to questions about their design choices. Socratic questioning is a type of prompt mentors use to pull information out of the mentee, to allow a student to hear themselves making propositions out loud. What exactly do mentors attempt to "pull" out of mentees? In project-based learning pipelines, learners can be prompted to:

- Explain how they are solving a problem

- Detail why they have decided to prioritize specific features

- Articulate a specific approach that helped the team remove an obstacle they had

- Take turns speaking out loud what the core idea of a project might be in within a specified time limit

- Identify which design-oriented tool will help them move the project forward

- Pitch innovative ideas or solutions for their projects without preparation

- Pitch ideas within specific time constraints, and often being challenged to pitch their ideas in shorter and shorter durations

Rather than giving the answer away or providing directives to learners, mentors apply this approach to stimulate the learner's imagination. They continually probe into the knowledge area with questions that are intended to move the state of the project forward, to draw attention to the team's biases, to bring awareness to the problem-solving process and identify what's missing, and so much more.

Socratic questioning also supports characteristics of self-regulatory behavior, such as critical thinking and self- reflection. In some cases, a mentor might prompt learners to identify their own lack of preparation through reflection, guide them toward a deeper understanding of why their team is not collaborating well, or help them talk aloud what they believe to be the root of the problem they are trying to solve. Socratic questioning requires patience on the part of the mentor. You need to develop the capacity to pose a question that is difficult to answer and wait in silence for learners to answer. Then, you can respond. You will benefit from practicing this out loud by having an internal count because when you are in the moment, you might think you have waited forever but only a second might have passed. The other approach is to just be silent until a student breaks that silence by answering. Sooner or later, someone will speak up.

Socratic questioning provokes an environment of strategic listening, where a mentor has learners talk first before they provide them with their opinion. It may also bring up unanticipated responses you did not expect and can challenge your ability to respond and support them, and in some cases reinforce their ideas, build on them instead of resisting their answer, or continuously probe for a "right" answer that is best for the team in the moment.

The answer that learners provide may not always be obvious and requires a Socratic approach to "root it out." On the simplest level, this process provides learners the opportunity to be heard. In hearing themselves speak, learners might better understand that they may know more than they realized, or they might learn how much of a struggle they have in articulating their ideas. Both contribute to increased self-understanding. For the mentor, the process can be an indicator as to how well an individual, a team, or the class is progressing. Learner responses to a prompt, or a lack of response, may point to the need for more formal teaching on the subject or additional team mentoring.

Allowing time for learners to answer in the form of propositions builds in them the capacity to listen to themselves and one another empowering them to also ask each other questions. This strategy is also related to the earlier one of modelling behavior to inspire learners to absorb an approach through practical experience rather than by solely reading about it.

In terms of the types of questions and how to form them, some questions can be considered leading questions. Other can be categorized as "recall questions," requiring learners to pause and take a moment to remember a tool or process taught and exercised earlier in the course that would help them solve the problem at hand. In most of the cases, learners will welcome the challenge and practice to be able to recall a specific tool, process, or visual map that they could apply to helping them solve the problem at hand.

Deeper Dive

Fischer, C. A. (2019). The power of the Socratic classroom. *Students. Questions. Dialogue. Learning.*

Learning Goals

In research conducted at the MDM Program, one mentor asked each individual team member, "What does 'good' look like at the end of the project?"

> *"They usually tell me from a team perspective and an individual perspective. And I keep that in mind to see if all the students are more or less aligned. And if they're all over the place that's fine because there's still plenty of time to align them, but also to see what their goals are … gives me a clue as to where they think they are at."*

While many professionals and learners don't always set explicit learning goals, they do have them. They just need to be articulated. The phrase "I would like to learn more about (fill in the blank)" is commonly heard in all types of technology development environments. Setting any type of goal is important as much research has shown. It's a way to direct the mind toward completing tasks that contribute to a goal. As a project management tool, Agile can support learners in breaking down what they need to accomplish in short-term tasks that contribute to an overall goal. The broader learning goal in this case can be "I would like to increase my knowledge of user interface design." One subgoal can be "decide with the team which color is best used in the UI to warn users of the dangers of having a short password."

The literature of mentoring and self-regulation both speak to the importance of goal setting, and numerous papers show that self-regulating learners improve academically when they set goals. Some research shows that learners who self-regulate also tend to search for new opportunities to learn, and in some cases, they are motivated to achieve more challenging goals for themselves. Some learning goals that students tend to articulate in PjBL environments include

- Improving their understanding of user experience design

- Gathering experience working on projects with other people

- Learning more about what makes technology work

- Gaining practical experience using Agile

- Learning how to create technology for others

- Solving wicked design problems

While students will have little problem with statements such as those written earlier, they will benefit from getting more specific, and you can help them with that by asking questions that challenge learners to provide more detail, give an example, etc. Take the first point as an example. A student might express that they wish to improve their understanding of user experience design. They might have heard of UX, and many previous instructors and students have spoken about its value but they may not know what actually goes into increasing knowledge and know-how of user experience design. Guiding questions like the ones that follow can help students clarify what aspect of UX design they want to learn more about, and this will also help you better inform you of what you may teach.

- What do you mean by UX design?

- What aspect of designing something for someone are you excited about?

- What types of human experiences are you interested in designing for with emerging technologies?

- What do you design?

Deeper Dive

Rožman, L., & Koren, A. (2013, June). Learning to learn as a key competence and setting learning goals. In *Proceedings of the Management, Knowledge and Learning International Conference* (pp. 19-21).

Group Genres

We are familiar with the term "genre" when it comes to understanding a particular style of music. There are film genres like horror, romantic comedy, fantasy, or action–adventure. There are also types of team practices that develop. These can be organized by the way the team approaches different aspects of project development over time. Some teams develop established practices or genres when it comes to developing products. Teams develop ways to collaborate, how to manage a project, how to use specific tools to complete tasks, and importantly, how to use structured practices to solve project, team, and client problems together. Each practice, each way of doing things can form part of their group genres.

How They Manifest

In the workplace, there will be many familiar tools and processes that team members draw from over time and practice. These are not always taught formally and there is an expectation for new recruits to "ramp up" their knowledge—to take responsibility for learning and practicing what they learn with team members. In a learning environment, these tools will need to be taught, and once the students apply them toward their projects, they transform into genres that are unique to the makeup to the team. While many of the tools that are taught beforehand can guide mentees toward solving specific design problems associated with the project that they work on, they need to be modified, refined, and at times completely reinvented for the context and problems that present themselves in a project.

Group genres will also manifest from group activities, methods that students learn and then apply, approaches to prototyping they engage in co-creating design thinking tools they adopt or abandon, etc. For example, teams will develop their own genre of Agile. In other words, it is a way of implementing Agile to manage their own context-specific projects together. They can also develop a way of implementing a design thinking tool like a Persona visual model to ensure they think of their audience or user in a particular way. How teams solve problems that come up together can point to a specific methodology. As PjBL teams start co-constructing a project together, they slowly start to develop a way of doing things.

Group genres can also be described as team *know-how* that comes from the *action of doing something together*. Genres develop and flow in the interplay of individuals collaborating to solve problems and in understanding who they are building their prototype for, fleshing out prototypes, and learning what they need to contribute to interdependent features. As the team generates their own ways of doing, they can draw from different group genres, even though a new design challenge manifests that may require a different approach. They modify the genre in action.

Mentor the Action of Doing

Mentoring will support learners in adapting something they just learned to the specific project that they engage in. Experience on multiple types of projects with different teams will also help support the type of feedback that you provide and give you a greater perspective for the unique ways of doing each team has.

All these emerging genres require mentoring. They ask you to be an active witness to how teams develop a project together, responding when necessary to support a team in improving that "way of doing things," which will help make that process more efficient, and at times complete. An example can be how a team uses a suite of design thinking tools and in what order. They may begin with a customer journey without first identifying who their potential customers are. They may invest a lot of time into developing personas that represent too wide a demographic for an application they are developing for teenagers. They may use a tool and not even know its purpose, nor why they are using it.

Mentors also bridge team genres that are emerging, with the problem that a team is trying to solve, knowing that each team member will bring a particular approach whose impulses are negotiated. At times this takes time as not all learners solve problems in the same way, and some may not have had enough experience with a particular tool or approach. How to solve a design challenge using a particular tool (e.g., the Bullseye) may be necessary for the mentor to model in the moment.

Mentors know that mentees can only solve contextual problems through the action of doing. They also know that not every individual in a group has the body of knowledge that might be required. This means that mentors need to facilitate individuals on a team to rely on each other to "fill in the blanks" where and when necessary. That knowledge can be elicited using Socratic questions as discussed previously. For example, if a team is working through a mind map that generates many ideas and directions the project can become, a mentor might ask, "Now that you have all these ideas, how might you prioritize them?". One team member might call up "with the bullseye." Another may offer "by determining which idea can best lead us to solving the problem the client identified."

Pausing for Reflection

Lastly, it's important to reflect with learners on how they approach solving a problem by making a proposition in the form of a prototype. Prototypes as a group genre activate a process where learners can assess the strengths and weaknesses of their combined individual efforts in the moment and when user-tested. Evaluating a tool or process that they use will help them determine if it becomes useful enough for the team to assimilate it as a group genre.

Deeper Dive

Cook, S. D., & Brown, J. S. (1999). Bridging epistemologies: The generative dance between organizational knowledge and organizational knowing. Organization science, 10(4), 381-400.

Scaffolding and Fading

> *"They were not either too much with us or too little. It was a good balance."*
>
> *"At the beginning they stayed longer with us. The first month every day and eventually less and less time with us."*
>
> *(Student responses to interviews in research that investigated supervisory practices)*

If you think of the purpose of a scaffold, it's to provide support for a person to climb higher and perform work while ensuring the structure they stand on is stable. This concept applies to learning as well. Students require foundational knowledge of what they need to know, to co-construct a project together.

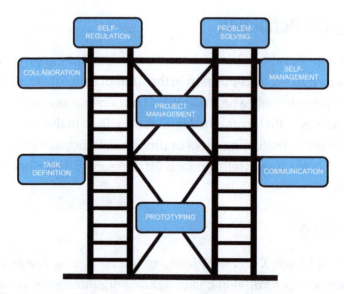

Figure 6-4. *Components of a PjBL pipeline that learners tend to need scaffolding for*

Figure 6-4 proposes several components of a PjBL pipeline where learners will more than likely need support. These include

- *Project management*: How to manage a project with a gradual fading of support, when it is communicated by a mentor at the beginning of a project cycle. An eventual team goal should be to manage their own work and the client by themselves.

- *Self-regulation*: How to manage their learning includes what they need to know to deliver tasks, how they will apply what they've learned to completing tasks, how they develop themselves within a collaborative environment, and more.

- *Prototyping*: How to prototype also means understanding the purpose of a prototype. This tasks learners to answer specific design questions they prepare in advance and validate through user testing.

- *Self-management*: How to manage their time, behaviors with other team members, and their mental well-being during stressful periods of time.

- *Task definition*: How to break down a feature into tasks, and work on identifying what's possible to achieve, what they need to learn to complete a task, prioritizing what task needs to be completed when, in relation to the work of other team members, and how much time it will take to complete a task, especially when others are depending on that task to complete theirs.

- *Problem-solving*: How to identify and solve problems together with others, which also includes deepening their understanding of the process through which they solve problems.

- *Collaboration*: How to collaborate well with others especially when the time they have to complete a project that they scoped shortens, and the pressure to deliver something tangible starts to affect the team.

- *Communication*: How to communicate effectively and persistently with other team members so that the team moves forward with their projects knowing what each team member is contributing, understanding the current Sprint goal of the project, and improving their communication style over time.

Importantly, to properly build these scaffolds, learners need to know why they need to learn all these interrelated parts that contribute toward prototyping an emerging technology project. Mentoring fits in by providing support to teams of learners on an as-needed basis. Research shows that as a team becomes more independent, they become more self-regulating, needing the mentor less.

In the setting of a project-based course, fading is part of a process that allows mentors to reduce their mentoring over time as students become increasingly self-reliant and team-reliant to solve problems that come up. Your goal as a mentor is to eventually fade into the distance and allow teams to self-govern. In doing so, learners organize and practice their developing self-competencies, and this can be amplified by taking on and performing different roles on projects.

No team is the same. Some teams may need more scaffolding over time than others, challenging any notion of consistent and pervasive fading across time and between teams. While the increase of mentoring may contradict a "natural" progression to fade, some interventions are necessary, according to previous research, as they contribute to greater self-determination and self-reliance from some members of the team.

Deeper Dive

Azevedo, R., & Hadwin, A. F. (2005). Scaffolding self-regulated learning and metacognition–Implications for the design of computer-based scaffolds. Instructional Science, 33(5), 367-379.

MacLeod, M., & van der Veen, J. T. (2020). Scaffolding interdisciplinary project-based learning: a case study. *European journal of engineering education, 45*(3), 363-377.

Productive Failure: Teams Solving Their Own Problems

"Sometimes they were just there sitting and listening.... Otherwise, they would not interrupt unless there was a struggle with something and they would suggest something, which doesn't mean what they were suggesting was the answer to our problems."

(Student interview from doctoral research)

In workplace environments just as in PjBL ones, mentors are often pressured with the choice between showing a mentee "how it's done," or letting mentees solve the problem for themselves. The stakes are different. Time is usually a factor in determining the approach. In an ideal situation, mentors won't solve problems for the mentees but rather encourage an environment where mentees themselves must iteratively approach solving problems on their own. With this approach, they become a witness to the mentee's articulation of their approach, process, and work—part of a regular feedback process for each iterative attempt mentees make to solve a project problem. Theoretically, that sounds great, but often on critical paths in workplace environments, there's not always the luxury of time when something needs to be released publically by a certain date.

When enacted in learning environments, productive failure affords learners a certain amount of time and effort to make mistakes, reflect on them, learn from them, and improve upon them as they generate the next solution to a design problem. You can decide whether you will intervene. What are the motivators that will provoke you to solve a problem for learners? What will hold you back from solving a problem for them?

Letting learners solve their own problems is a key feature of both PjBL environments and the learning outcome of self-regulation. The positioning echoes the research in the literature of supporting an environment whereby mentees are expected to rely upon themselves to initiate, problem solve, and move the state of the project forward rather than to rely on external motivation to be told what to do. There are, of course, moments where you as a mentor must intervene if a project is going to be "derailed," especially if mentees need outside mitigation of an irresolvable interpersonal problem between team members.

Reinventing Failure in PjBL Environments

In emerging tech development, the saying "fail fast, fail often" is often heard. Yet operationalizing what failure means is not widely practiced. There may be an assumption as to what it means but not everyone will have the same sentiment. In learning environments, you will need to define what you mean by failure and it would benefit all the students to do the same. You will likely find a lot of negative attributes to the word, laced with fear, apprehension, uncertainty, and a feeling of being judged. The meaning of "failure" is often associated with not passing a course in academic environments, so the concept needs to completely reimagined with learner input and reflection.

After expressing all the negative definitions of the word, it will be easier to recalibrate what failure can mean in the context of product development. To reinvent the process of creating something for another human, that upon being tested, challenges the assumptions a team might have made about the experience it would provide. Thus, productive failure becomes something to strive to experience, a critical part of the iterative process of creation. Productive failure is a process, a group genre to attain, a mindset of experimentation and testing leading to the continuous improvement of a designed human experience.

> *"I think that also in order for them to improve they have to have something to contrast it. So they know this was a bad meeting. Maybe that will stimulate them in their next meeting to be more on the ball. Failure is a learning opportunity."*
>
> *(Mentor during an interview about a failed client meeting)*

Cycles of productive failure can be tolerated when using Agile as a project management methodology in PjBL environments. This is especially true when productive failure is associated with taking risks and is rewarded.

Client interactions afford learners many opportunities for productive failure as they will often make mistakes during meetings with the client. Mentors can identify behaviors that may have been unclear or disagreed with the client, discuss the meeting's design, and reflect how the team communicated. This will help the team to better understand why a meeting turned out in a particular way, the consequences of their behaviors and communication habits, and how they could prevent future errors from recurring. Allowing learners to make mistakes during a client meeting can be tolerated to a certain extent. Important is to call out certain behaviors with the client present with grace and humor.

Memorable Stories

There was once a beautiful fish that lived in a pond near a village. For as long as people could remember, pilgrimages were taken to visit the fish. All who saw the fish were transfixed by its beauty. The great god Shiva heard of the fish and decided to pay her a visit. Shiva was transfixed by the fish's eyes. In those eyes Shiva saw the history of humankind, its stories, its tragedies, its comedies. The deeper Shiva looked into the magical fish's eyes the more stories were revealed. Soon all the stories of every single person to have ever lived were made known. Then, the last story revealed itself and as Shiva saw itself watching and listening to stories being told by a fish in a pond, it disappeared into the eyes of the fish. To this day, to the best of my knowledge the fish is still there, but no one is quite sure where the pond can be found.

(Adapted from Sufi Story)

Storied experiences resonate with learners. It's important to tell them and practice doing so. Think of stories that are short, memorable, and impactful that happened to you in any type of development pipeline. How might these relate to what learners are currently facing? When stories are recounted in the context of mentoring learners on projects, they provide them with a perspective of "how it's been done before"; what the faculty mentor did when faced with a similar situation, problem, or challenge. That story makes the associated lesson learned more memorable. Timing of a story is important. You can't force stories, but when you believe the situation at hand would benefit from one, they can make the experience more memorable, especially when told with humility and vulnerability.

Based on research with professional mentors, memorable stories tend to be present at every stage of a PjBL pipeline. These are stories that usually recount the challenges you have experienced in a typical production. Stories can be about anything from team collaboration, pipeline, dependencies, clients, project pivots, problem-solving, and management. The following story speaks to the value of bringing an agenda to a client meeting.

> *Once upon a time at the beginning of the very first client meeting, students did not outline an agenda so the client took over the agenda guiding the team toward what she wanted. The result was that the team did not convey all they wanted to and felt like the client had taken over the project. We discussed the value of having an objective to the meeting as well as an agenda and the team was reminded of a specific organizational tool they had all learned and failed to apply. They understood its value and set up the next meeting. Upon the start of that next meeting, the team started in the same way as before, without objective or agenda, but this time before I could intervene, the client without missing a beat said, "Would you like me to take over the meeting again or do you want to own this project?"*

To Do: Write Out Your Memorable Stories

Drawing from your storybook is an organic process that a particular situation with learners may trigger. What are memorable stories you tell and in what situations would you tell them? What stories do you remember the most that were told to you when you were on a project team? Which stories have you told team members and for what reasons? Think about an incident or experience you had in workplace that might make for a memorable story and write it down. Create a small collection as you may draw upon these in different situations so making them explicit by writing them down is the first part of helping you to recall them.

Managing Client or Proxy Client

If clients form part of the experience you wish learners to have in the PjBL environment that you design, they add a whole other area of management. As a mentor, you need to balance their expectations with those of your students. Mentoring learners to manage the client's expectations can involve the following:

- *Deciphering the language that clients use to communicate their ideas*: At times, this requires translation because the team may need help in assimilating a client's use of specific vocabulary and this terminology tends to belong to the community of practice they are a part of. This is most effective directly after a client meeting because memories are fresh, and you spend time reflecting with the students.

- *Helping the students to eliminate some of the communication barriers will lead to less misunderstanding, time wasted, and stress*: Paying attention to the client's use of vocabulary also makes learners exercise a more focused listening. Teaching them when it is appropriate to interrupt a client, how to do so gracefully, and stay with the agenda can also relieve a lot of stress and make meetings short.

- *Reinventing clients as partners in the project's co-construction*: Often, learners are under the impression that they must make propositions at every phase of production that needs approval from a client vs. providing a status update of the project. If you as mentor set up the relationship between client and learners as a partnership and communicate this to the client before first contact, then it proposes different Rules of Play. Those rules include involving the client in initial brainstorming activities and drawing from the client or their employees as a resource. This approach improves the overall project and brings the client in on any design decisions and processes.

- *Negotiating the scope of a project based on the amount of time the learners will have on it*: Learners new to production tend to over scope ideas. They have an idea of what they could do and want to overachieve and please a client. A scoping tool like the What IF visual model, which is detailed in Appendix 1, can help prioritize what the team could deliver. A visual model like this allows learners to blue-sky ideas and to consider those they believe they can achieve. As mentor, you would moderate what is achievable or even what features are possible vs. those that would be "nice-to-haves," if the team has sufficient time to complete them.

- *Working with clients to accurately identify a problem to be solved*: This may involve several brainstorming sessions where the team and client can be facilitated to use a root cause visual model, such as the five Whys. This is because often a client is confident with what they want, but not as clear as to what their users need. That distinction is important to highlight when engaging learners in the beginning of a co-construction process. Asking "why?" persistently at this phase of ideation can help the client and team get closer to identifying the problem to be solved.

- *Persistently engaging in communication with the client*: This includes developing a remote and written communication style that is concise to minimize the client's time commitment in-between classes. Learners will also benefit from updating their clients as to how the project is progressing on a weekly basis. At the beginning of a project, they need to agree with the client on a Rule of Play that affords persistent as-needed communication, especially as they attempt to better grasp what they will co-construct together and the problem the project's prototype will solve.

At times mentors might also role-play as client, providing the team an opportunity to test out propositions with the mentor enacting how the client might respond. This is useful for learners to be able to understand the impact of their propositions and even how they communicate them. Often, it is how an idea is communicated that has an impact on how well it is received, no matter how great that idea might be.

Listening

> *"There is a sense of composure when they are around. They have an incredible ability to listen...to let team talk when it needs to but also, they have an incredible sense of not letting the conversation divert completely."*
>
> *(Student interview discussing their supervisor)*

One of the most challenging mentoring strategies for mentors and teachers generally is to know when to stop talking and start listening. When mentoring on PjBL courses, mentors use listening as a strategy and encourage learners to listen to themselves, become aware as to how they listen to others, and shift from wanting to get their two cents in to responding to other team members. Mentoring learners to become better at listening to one another is a constant strategy that affects all other strategies. By listening, you model a learner's capacity to listen, and in so doing, challenge them to be present and focused on the mentoring session. Mentoring learners to improve their listening can be activated in many ways. One strategy is tasking learners to articulate a state of the project they are working on, provide them feedback, and then have them try again to see if they heard you. Mentors actively listen to guide a conversation or lab session from drifting away from the subject completely.

You may also anticipate that learners may simply be seeking affirmation for their ideas or efforts. When you do, you can apply a three-step process.

- Draw attention to their intent by first affirming that they are all brilliant and that feedback cycles are part of a core value in your learning environment that is focused on continuous improvement.

- Affirm a learner's intelligence first and can then be followed by reminding them that their propositions

can always be improved upon, and that the process of
improvement happens in professional environments
just as regularly.

- Provide them honest feedback on their ideas and
  repeat that they will benefit from understanding that it
  is the ideas you are providing feedback on, not on the
  individuals who created those ideas.

Everyone wants their ideas to be loved, appreciated, or at least
affirmed. It's important to bring their attention to what their expectations
of others are when they present ideas, and their responses to criticism,
as the patterns may also be repeated with clients. As a strategy, listening
intently to learners allows you to provide them feedback not just on their
ideas, but on how they are expressing them, as an attempt to build their
confidence, affirm their intelligence, avoid harmful and unnecessary
evaluations of self-worth. Talking through how their communication style
might also trigger responses from others is useful feedback for them to
hear. For example, one team presented their ideas as "the most innovative"
and "the best solution" when a quick Google search revealed that, in fact,
their ideas were not unique and had been tried before. Providing tips on
how to present ideas will benefit learners in these moments to ensure they
are receiving valuable feedback on the ideas themselves, not on how they
were presented.

You can also create Rules of Play (Appendix 1) around your mentoring
style when you create a contract with learners. One that comes to mind
to state is that you are not there to love their ideas, but to challenge
them in believing in the value proposition of their ideas. Or, that you are
interrogating the idea not them. This keeps learners from relying on the
mentor to make decisions for them. Listening to learners will also uncover
what they are thinking and feeling. This helps mentors better understand
how the team is progressing with a project and the course content.
Facilitating learners to create Rules of Play around how they would like

to give and receive feedback is also helpful in getting them to appreciate differences and include these rules in their working agreements. Calling out stereotypical feedback styles like the contentious "shit sandwich" or other methods you or your mentors have accepted is also important to address. The purpose of feedback is also to learn how to improve how it might be received and thus reinvent the feedback process itself, creating a safe and healthy feedback environment.

Listening can also be supported by encouraging learners to capture ideas visually. There is value in doing so as it is difficult to remember all the ideas that are generated on a team. Facilitating some of the techniques that you have used can support this habit. One is the use of capturing minutes, or short form, bullet point notes on what is said in a meeting. This is an effective tool to use during client meetings to ensure that what was discussed is captured and then sent as a document to keep track of requirements, and to confirm with clients that everything that was written down accurately reflects the captured conversation. Using a variety of different visual models that help to organize ideas is another method and encourages learners to think and organize their ideas in visual containers. For example, if a team is brainstorming a bunch of ideas about the most important themes that their story is going to address, a nodal system can be designed, such as a mind map, where the words "important themes" are placed in the middle of a whiteboard or page with a circle drawn around it, and thematic ideas can be brainstormed connecting to the central node through a line drawn toward it.

Organize Your Own Mentoring Strategies

There are many mentoring strategies you have likely used in professional settings. Some may be like the ones shown in the previous section of this chapter. Others may not have been covered that you engage in regularly. The following process is intended to help you organize your strategies under specific categories.

Identify Your Mentoring Strategies

Identify the methods or strategies that you use. Draw from the previous ones offered, but importantly, use as many words to describe each mentoring strategy. The following process and example can be used. Read through it and then fill in your own words in order to develop your own personal style. Identify what methods you are comfortable with and which you want to explore to challenge your own comfort zone.

Step 1: Identify your own strategies.

Use the following first sentence and fill it in with your own words.

When I mentor others at work, I find that

_____

- Talking through things really helps.
- Repeating the same message daily is helpful.
- Getting them to talk through a problem is effective.
- Listening first shows that I am thoughtful and not trying to tell.
- I spend a lot of time showing people where to go to find an answer.
- Demonstrating how to do something is fastest.
- Inspiring individuals on teams helps buy-in.
- Humor helps to break the ice.

Step 2: Attribute a one- or two-word value to each sentence. (This has been done for the preceding sentences.)

- Explaining

- Repeating

- Talking through

- Listening

- Guiding

- Demonstrating

- Inspirating

- Using humor

Step 3: Organize your strategies on a bullseye. Using a bullseye helps you to map the ones you use more than others.

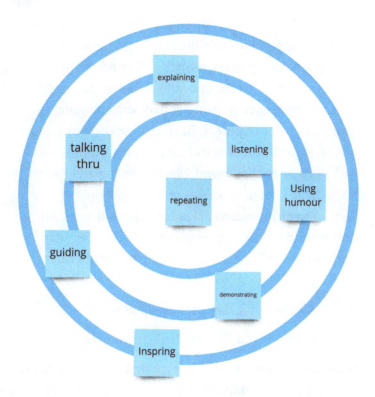

Figure 6-5. *Clustered and prioritized mentoring strategies*

Balancing Between Individual and Group Mentoring

When mentoring is spontaneous, it can happen so quickly that it's difficult to map who the mentoring was directed toward, particularly in team-based co-creation. It's also a challenge to measure the impact your mentoring has had on the team and the project itself.

There are many conditions that will inform the balance between individual and group mentoring. These include:

- Team size

- Scope of project

- Level of experience individuals have on the team with previous pipelines. Assigning individuals to teams should also take into consideration the level of experience each person has had with emerging technology development. Balance is not easy to achieve in this regard. Students with much more experience will need to be challenged. Placing them with less experienced team members may compel them to lead or to be pressured to lead by other students. All this should be talked through with more experienced individuals and additional learning outcomes can also be set.

- Level of experience the team itself has together.

- How open individuals are to being mentored.

The pendulum in Figure 6-6 depicts a swinging state for the mentor between mentoring individuals one-on-one, individuals while on a team, and all individuals at the same time.

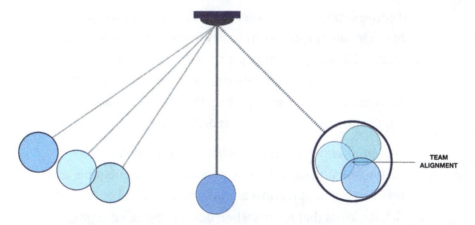

Figure 6-6. *Mentor in the center of the image balances mentoring between a team of individuals on the right with individuals on the left*

Spontaneous Mentoring As a Known Unknown

Mentors may have a wide variety of intentions when they meet with teams. Because of the organic flow of project-based development, however, there are many times when a planned meeting can take place and the mentor does not have any goals except to check in. Those circumstances provoke mentors to spontaneously respond to student work in progress. Mentoring in this capacity is something you can expect to engage in. While meeting with teams, you may need to respond to the following known unknowns:

- *Questions or confusion that mentees might have about the process*: This may not always be communicated but some of the signs can be a misunderstanding of how to use a design thinking tool, not knowing where they might in the production pipeline, and not always being able to evaluate the quality of their work accurately due to a lack of experience.

- *The application of tools that mentees have been asked to use to solve problems*: You may encounter teams engaged in storyboarding the user experience, for example, and notice that they did not take into account what motivated a user to pick up the device and use the application they are in process of designing.

- *Design-oriented questions such as scope, pipeline, etc.*: Ad hoc mentoring will play a persistent role in helping learners understand how to under promise and over deliver. What that means when developing an emerging technology project is to support learners to not promise too many features, excel at them, and if there is time, include some that were in "nice-to-have."

- *Reflection and/or reaction on the current "playable" state of the project*: Students will want to explain before you try their playable prototypes, and it is important to stop that impulse and try the prototype first, give them your impression, and then have them add any explanations or context afterward. Your mentoring may likely be focused on the user experience and "ease of use" of the application they are developing.

- *Team communication and collaborative issues that may have surfaced as the team approaches solving problems together*: At times, mentors enter a room in which a battle or argument may have happened. Trust your sense and read of the room in terms of understanding the tension that might be present. Always have some type of resolution tool at your disposal as students on most project teams will eventually have disputes or disagreements that can easily escalate. In this regard, you become more than just a moderator. Your goal should always be to find the source of the problem, articulate what you think it is, listen to learner responses, then and provide them with a path toward equitable resolution.

- *If the project is client-based, questions you ask the team can center around what a client might ask*: You may also find it useful to embody the client and respond as they might to a particular pitch, prototype, or change (pivot) in the project purpose and intent that the students propose.

Targeting Project, Team, and Client

In a PjBL environment, you will always be challenged to prioritize what's most important to teach and mentor in the moment, as a response to the team that's in front of you. That can make it chaotic to determine what you should engage with. To help organize your teaching and mentoring, focus on three intersecting domains that learners need to manage: how they manage themselves, their assigned project, and their relationship with clients.

Figure 6-7. *Target the objective of a mentoring strategy to how the team manages their collaboration together, how they manage the client, or how they manage the project pipeline*

The Project

Targeting the mentoring to the project itself can encompass execution, tasks, timeline, scope, finding support for task completion, prototyping, and management.

The Team

Mentoring strategies can be organized around the team's evolving individual and group needs. This includes their collaboration, communication patterns, problem-solving process, how they align to make decisions together, the methods they use to prioritize, team and individual goal setting, Rules of Play governing their behavior toward one another, buy-in to the project and client, and sustaining an equitable culture.

The Client

Targeting mentoring to improve client relations can be focused on how students interact with the client, how they create boundaries, how they present their ideas, how they respond to client challenges, how they mitigate the client's use of subclients, how present a client is during a production pipeline, and how they persistently scope the client's asks over the course of the project.

When clients are integrated into the course and learners have to manage them, they are best reinvented as partners in PjBL. This approach allows learners the opportunity to increase a client's overall buy-in to a project. The reinvention of a client as partner also allows the potential for:

- Increased pace of decision-making allowing more tasks and therefore a prototype with an increased number of features to be delivered

- Less of a proposition or pitch-based project at every phase and one that is more inherently collaborative

- Improved communication and alignment

- A deeper relationship with clients and teams to be made

- Learners more potential touchpoints with the client's circle of employees and communities of practice.

Balancing Attention to the Three Zones

Exactly how mentees manage themselves, the project, and the client is different from case to case. That "how" depends on many factors, including a mentee's previous professional experience, their maturity, the type of project it is, and the client's personality and expectations. A mentee's management of these three intersecting zones, however, is not linear. Attention and care must be dispersed to each zone depending on how much management needs to occur. Mentors need to balance their attention of these three areas and give them equal weight. Mentees for the most part intuitively understand that managing these intersecting zones remains top of mind. Nevertheless, there is a persistent ask from mentees to be given a template, a how-to, an order of things that they need to do to start to co-construct a digital prototype. And this is one of the problems for any mentor engaged in managing their interactions with mentees within a project-based learning environment. There is no singular way. There is no precise how-to, which makes PjBL exciting and challenging at the same time.

Chapter Summary

Those strategies will come in handy as you begin to see how they can be applied to supporting the core features that manifest in PjBL environments in the next chapter.

This chapter

- Dove into the types of mentoring strategies that are common in PjBL environments

- Gave specific examples of mentoring strategies and tasked you to relate to some of them as to-dos

- Suggested that you begin to identify your own

Tools and Suggested Processes

- When mentoring, target the objective of a mentoring strategy to how the team manages their collaboration together, how they manage the client, or how they manage the project pipeline.

- Identify your mentoring strategies in the workplace through a three-step process that includes fully describing the strategy, condensing that strategy to one or two words and then mapping them on a bullseye model to differentiate between those that you use more and those that you use less.

Deeper Dive

Healy, C. C., & Welchert, A. J. (1990). Mentoring relations: A definition to advance research and practice. *Educational Researcher, 19*(9), 17-21.

Parsloe, E. (1992). Coaching, mentoring, and assessing: A practical guide to developing competence. Nichols Publishing Company.

Whitehead, J., & Fitzgerald, B. (2006). Professional learning through a generative approach to mentoring: Lessons from a training school partnership and their wider implications. *Journal of Education for Teaching, 32*(1), 37-52.

Wong, A.T., Premkumar, K. (2007). An Introduction to Mentoring Principles, Processes, and Strategies for Facilitating Mentoring Relationships at a Distance

Klasen, N., & Clutterbuck, D. (2012). Implementing mentoring schemes. Routledge.

CHAPTER 7

Know the Core Features of PjBL

Chapter Goal: This chapter proposes that designers of PjBL courses consider core features that are common when learners develop emerging technology projects together. Understanding these core features will lead to improving the design of learning that integrates important competencies associated with each.

To inform your design of a PjBL course

You need to group what students need to learn in categories of core competencies

So you can develop learning outcomes that students will take away from the course.

> *The last time I lectured for more than ten minutes advocating for project-based courses in post-secondary curriculum, no matter what the discipline, was at a conference for continuing legal educators in San Diego. To be fair, I was asked to present on a big stage with a fairly large audience that was far away. I found out afterward that I had been hyped by a colleague who invited me to be the keynote that this was going to be unlike anything they ever experienced before. That when they experienced me teach it was a fiesta, filled with colored balls, group split-offs and overall what was to them, a highly interactive environment. Instead, I lectured. I lectured because I*

© Patrick Parra Pennefather 2022
P. Parra Pennefather, *Mentoring Digital Media Projects*,
https://doi.org/10.1007/978-1-4842-8798-9_7

listened to the needs of the organizer who said something like "Well, this is what our keynotes usually do. They speak. They talk about what they do and provide takeaways." So my one-hour lecture, my talk, my whatever it was with tons of slides and rehearsed sequences was filled with tools that the audience could apply in their classrooms to increase interaction. It went over like one of those dull moments we've all had in a lecture hall, head nodding off and on, really really long, never knowing when it would end. At least that was what I felt like. By the time Q&A hit, I couldn't wait to get off stage and lead a parade or something. Just as time was running out and the crickets became a bit more audible in the room, one person at the back called out "So none of what you said today is unknown to me." And faster than a whip, a front row attendee in their early twenties responded: "Yes the only difference is that you never actually implemented anything interactive in the classes you taught." Woah. Awkward silence, then laughter and cheers from an audience who I imagine were all familiar with the critic at the back of the room.

What you learn in this book needs to be applied to make sense to both you and learners. When you teach in a post-secondary institution, anticipate that some learners will prefer the lecture and some will want to engage in the doing. PjBL is a feedback engine that requires the student's voices in the mix to constantly make the experience better. So you design with that in mind. You design to maximize the experience of doing, and integrate theory or how-tos that are then applied in the 'doing of'.

Beyond the hard skills that are required to contribute to a project, the specifics of what students need to experience can be organized within larger categories. Once identified, these larger categories, or core features of PjBL, can then be more easily associated with competencies that form part of the learner experience. Taking time to focus on these core features will support you in developing targeted activities that reinforce robust learning outcomes. This chapter will outline those features and provide some examples of how you can activate each feature within your instructional design with experiential activities. Figure 7-1 represents a set of common core features you can consider designing for in PjBL environments.

Figure 7-1. *Core features of PjBL to integrate into your design*

Design for Learning Creativity

Designing your learning environment to allow learners to exercise their creativity involves planning activities that facilitate learners to become more aware of their creative process and how to negotiate that creativity with others. While creativity is exercised throughout a PjBL pipeline, the *"Discovery"* phase, as the word portrays, is the beginning part of a project where learners uncover ideas based on a specific prompt: the project brief. The ideas that they uncover emerge from a brainstorming process where they can apply a series of ideation tools to help frame their creative explorations (see Appendix 1). Specific tools are applied to help them create boundaries around what they think is possible and what might not be doable when considering the skills they have, what they would need to learn to complete tasks associated with a project, and the amount of time they are willing to commit to the course. Within and throughout the course, learners begin to understand who they are designing a solution for. Each project brief implies a potential target user or human and learners can use several human-centered design tools (Appendix 1) to deepen their understanding of who they will make their final prototype for. As they will encounter numerous problems related to the project, their collaborations with each other and a client partner, there will be no shortage of opportunities to propose solutions, receive feedback on them; refine them, and then propose more new solutions.

Project Brief

Exercising creativity begins at the outset of the course. A learner's imagination is jump-started upon reading and interpreting a Project Brief that helps them direct their creativity toward solving a human problem through the development of prototypes. The benefits of having learners take on a project that is not their own include the negotiation of scope, time, aesthetic, and ideas in collaboration with an external client. In a way, it's easier for student not used to developing their own original product ideas to have a member of a community of practice propose one. The following process can be followed:

- After learners are given a summary of expectations and access to a course outline, they are introduced to a one- or two-page document that explains the initial brief. That brief can detail the type of project, the sought-after technological medium, a theme, and a potential target user or audience and can even identify a problem that the project might solve.

- Following receipt of a Brief, the student team is asked to conduct research of the client or faculty partner and the type of project the client is interested in. Some of that research can investigate who has done similar projects in the past, whether similar problems have been solved differently, the affordances and constraints the technology offers those who will use it, and the type of skills that would be required to pull it off. While learners start to brainstorm ideas, they also being to understand what roles they might want to play and identify what they would need to learn to complete tasks associated with those roles.

- From a first encounter with a brief, many questions will also be brainstormed as it is important to understand the client partner's motivation and why they would want to use a specific technology to solve the problem they've highlighted for their targeted users. In the process of asking questions, learners may also uncover root cause problems that were not identified in the brief. For this reason, it is important to meet with the client partner early, designing accelerators with them, in order to move the state of the project forward so the team can start prototyping.

Brainstorming

Essential to all project co-construction is to create a space where learners can feel safe and thus make increasingly risky offers. Don't take for granted that learners have experience brainstorming. Maybe some have not been encouraged in previous educational experiences to exercise their creativity or develop and share ideas. Some learners might have been judged for sharing ideas and may now resist doing so. Other learners may believe that they are not creative at all.

I never knew I had permission to come up with crazy ideas until I took your course. I finally feel like I have a platform to share ideas and it didn't matter if my team went with it or not. It was great to just get them out of my head.

(Excerpt from student evaluation of a course, with permission)

Regardless of the *Persona (Appendix 1)* that comes to the brainstorming session, one of your responsibilities is to facilitate open and persistent brainstorming at every phase of a production pipeline. Reflect on your own brainstorming experiences and how you or others contributed to co-creating a safe environment where ideas could be shared openly. A discussion of the brainstorming process would also benefit students so they learn and practice sharing blue-sky ideas in addition to refining and scoping those ideas to tangible ones they think they are capable of transforming into a deliverable proof-of-concept prototype.

To assist you and learners, it is helpful to draw up *Rules of Play* around the sharing of ideas prior to just jumping in. These are similar to the *Rules of Play* visual model as discussed previously. *Rules of play* around brainstorming give learners the freedom to explore and do so in a safe environment where their ideas will not be judged negatively. As a mentor, you will need to facilitate some interactions, and if a student strays from the *Rules of Play*, you need to draw attention to it and then remind them of the rules they have come up with as a team.

Visual models act as containers to make ideas visible and shared. They also focus brainstorming within certain boundaries. For example, simple nodal diagrams can be created if you are using a mind map–like model and place a central idea in the center node and then ask learners to brainstorm ideas generated from that single concept or idea. There are dozens of visual models that help to guide the direction of a brainstorm for specific purposes. Figure 7-2 and the accompanying journal article showing the value of brainstorming bad ideas in the "Deeper Dive" section are worth reviewing to understand the benefits of facilitating students to think about generating bad ideas in the form of features that are related to their projects.

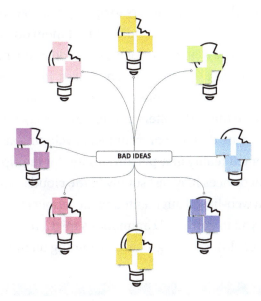

Figure 7-2. Another model where students can explore Bad Ideas and cluster those that are similar within grouped nodes

Ideation Tools

Common ideation tools in emerging tech projects include the following:

- Human-centered oriented ones such as a *Persona* visual model, day in the life, or other storyboarding tools to help learners better articulate their assumptions of potential users/audiences/customers visually.

- Node-based maps such as the mind map described in the previous example. *Context maps* are another example of a type of visual model that can help learners define the user flow based on actions they may or may not take, resulting in different outcomes.

- Landscape-oriented visual models help to structure ideas within visual metaphors that can sometimes make the experience more memorable. A *What IF* visual model allows learners to openly brainstorm ideas no matter how big and then plot them on an x,y plane. The higher they place their ideas, the more time it will take to create. In some cases, ideas may be impossible to achieve, but it's important to let learners know as to make the offers as these may trigger new ones that are doable. For example, developing an augmented reality first-person shooter for multiple types of devices may rest solidly in the clouds, whereas using a web-based augmented reality application that allows you to embed 3D animations might rest in the center or closer to the ground depending on the scope.

Figure 7-3. *What IF map allows team members to offer ideas that range from less difficult to achieve at the bottom of the model to ideas that are more complex and will likely take more time at the top*

Scoping Tools

One of the biggest challenges that teams face is to properly scope a project. In other words, accurately estimate how long it will take to realize an idea as a functional prototype that their team can build together within a certain period of time. The problem is that most learners have no idea how long a fully featured interactive technology prototype will take to build. Mentors need to allow learners to aim for *blue-sky* thinking, in addition to brainstorming small-scale ideas. What's helpful is to conduct exercises where learners are tasked to break down features from user stories that uncover user needs. After this, they can prioritize the features that emerge from user stories on a *bullseye* visual model (Appendix 1) and then better prioritize what's possible.

Solving Problems First

A gap that is often seen in the development of digital media products, particularly those driven by an identified need or problem to be solved, is where a team should begin their ideation from. The team might ask: "Are we building a mobile application, some kind of interactive HTML5 site, the vertical or horizontal slice of an AR mobile game?" It's difficult but necessary to say to learners to not focus on the medium first, but to focus on which medium will best solve the identified problem for the targeted user. The pros and cons of using a variety of media to solve a problem should also be discussed. In addition, the idea of being creative about understanding the different touchpoints a user will have with the medium should be highlighted. A key tool to achieve this is storyboarding.

Developing a Visual Vocabulary

When learners unfamiliar with collaborative design processes try and be creative together, offers tend to remain in the world of conversation until one or more learners say something like "we should probably take notes." Learners from across disciplines tend not to be trained in capturing their ideas visually. They will be more used to note-taking using words, bullet points, and on occasion complementary doodling, which is probably more common in different types of creative workspaces.

Learners may have a strong conceptual sense of their ideas but will not really know how well they apply until they are made tangible, until they begin to prototype. This is where the application of various types of visual models can be extremely useful. There are many different types of containers such as maps and visual models that help capture a variety of ideas and become a stronger imprint to remind teams of a creative session they might have had. These contribute toward a visual vocabulary, a Group Genre (Chapter 6) that they can draw from when new creative challenges emerge. A common one is a mind map, where a central idea lives in the middle of a page and lines come out of it joining to new nodes or bubbles that explore associated ideas. There are dozens of other graphic organizers such as concept maps that show ideas within nodes whose ideas are connected with lines and arrows that are labeled with words that link words together and often explain how they are connected.

Design for Humans

It is common practice for teams to want to make something that they think will be amazing but not that useful to any human. With beginners, often the intention is to make something "cool" that will show off their portfolio. It's critical to emphasize that when something is designed, it has purpose and trade-offs. Design is different than an artistic process in that it is primarily focused on improving the human experience, solving a problem, or fulfilling a need. New problems may also emerge as students undertake their design process. Teaching learners to get used to the idea of designing for humans is a persistent theme and a necessary feature of the design of learning.

Throughout the design process, student teams need to be guided to make something useful for their user, and test their assumptions. A common way to do so is by persistently trying to define who the prototype will be for. Mapping out a potential target demographic persona or several and visualizing a day in the life of a typical user in order to locate points of interaction can also be helpful in determining a list of features a product might have. This is another important reason to focus on a human-centered design particularly one that's in its prototypical first stages.

Interaction Patterns

Another part of designing for humans is to map out the types of interactions that are expected of them. This helps the team begin to think of how their imagined user will use their interactive prototype. There are several actions learners can take that will influence what they prototype.

- Defining the physical action a user must take to interact with your product is a valuable idea, whether through a touch screen, ancient mouse, or speech to text.

- Defining the constraint is equally valuable. Use of right hand only. Use of both hands gesturally. Use of voice and hands on keyboard, etc. Are they considering accessibility or neurodivergence when they begin their design process?

- Considering the cyclic use and duration of engagement with the prototype. Is it an interaction that demands a lot of time from the participants? Is it a five-minute mobile game or a one-hour time-suck? How often will the users interact and when is an ideal time to capture their attention with your product? Also, how quickly can someone get a response from the interaction, both initially as in how long they wait for an application to start or a machine to turn on?

- Addressing competing attention factors. What are those possible distractions in life that will prevent someone from interacting with what the team builds? Can they build something that can be integrated into a daily routine? Or is what they are building an add-on to life's already busy activities? How important can it be in someone's daily routine? How does the process affect their cognitive load?

- Imagining the type of engagement. In other words, is the interaction of practical use like a calendar that reminds someone to look? Is it a game that improves brain activity? Is it an application that pushes out a daily meme to brighten someone's day based on settings they input? Is it a language lesson to enhance learning? These questions can also be turned into statements to constrain scope and discover an ideal target interaction.

- Determining mediation. How many layers of mediation exist between one human and other living humans through the technology? These can be mapped ranging from low mediation when interacting with

unnetworked artificial intelligence to high engagement
interactions via a video conferencing application,
open source or proprietary software that can appear as
virtual cameras allowing more effects and animations
to be layered with the original video feed.

Psycho-Demographic Profiling

Teaching and mentoring learners to always keep who they are designing
for top of mind is an important component in the overall experience of a
PjBL course. There are many tools that can be facilitated to achieve this
goal, from a variety of design traditions.

Personas are part of a large body of visual models that can be
organized under psycho-demographic or psychographic profiles, which
represent a potential product user, who they are, their habits, and what
they might need. Learners need to be aware of the dangers of profiling,
reinforcing stereotypes, which can limit and in some cases prohibit the
potential audience. It may be more strategic to develop personas based on
likes and dislikes and other criteria that any gender identity can relate to.

Figure 7-4. A persona map of a potential user or customer on a video
conferencing application

Storyboarding

Applying storyboarding, which, is common to comics, graphic novels, and film, storyboarding can help break down different touchpoints that a user might have with a prototype a team is co-constructing. A Day in the Life storyboard projects all the potential interaction points a user might have with the product in a typical day. Customer journeys may not look like typical storyboards, but they essentially tell a story of how a potential user finds out about a product, tries it, and is motivated to continue its use over time. Journey mapping can also bridge a Persona that a team has identified. Any aspect of the design process can be storyboarded as it challenges learners to break down all the assumptions they might have of their projected user, including what is being asked of users.

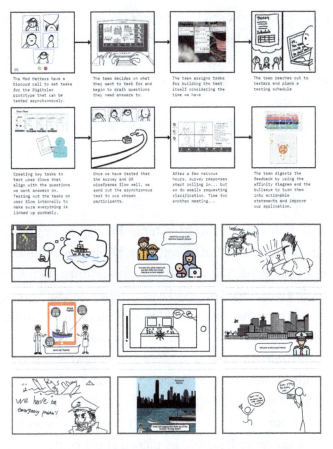

Figure 7-5. *Two types of storyboards used for different projects by students at the MDM Program in Vancouver, Canada*

User Stories in Agile

Guiding learners early through a user-centered approach to identify certain features that the prototype will consist of over a specified period will help them better scope what's possible. Teaching teams to apply User Stories, common to Agile methodologies, will support learners in defining the needs of a potential user they've decided their prototype will be made for. For example, *as an* eighteen-year-old, *I want* to post pictures of my friends *so I can* show the world how popular I am. Teaching the format of user stories also helps learners decompose larger features that a user need implies into smaller interdependent tasks that team members can then prioritize over time. This process can reveal assumptions that team members make about what it takes to deliver a feature or even a task, which leads to increased clarity on what a person is promising to deliver over a specified period.

Prioritization

There are many types of prioritization tools that can be implemented throughout the development of a prototype. Some like a Bullseye map can support learners in highlighting the must-have or must-include features when developing a project. Others like the MoSCoW 2 by 2 grid can be used to narrow down what is absolutely necessary when a product is released. A Bullseye map is an effective way to prioritize any idea or feature of a prototype to help the team and client focus on what is most important to the user. Bullseye maps can be usually visualized with three concentric circles much like a standard dart board. Ideas or features are placed on individual sticky notes, and the greater the priority of that feature being co-constructed, the more it should be placed at the center of the bullseye. Those features that are less important for the client and team of learners are placed on the outer rings. Typical questions teams of learners ask to help guide how they prioritize features include the following:

- How critical is the feature to the overall user experience?

- Which features are must-haves, and which are could-haves? Which are unnecessary at this time?

- Which features can be created later?

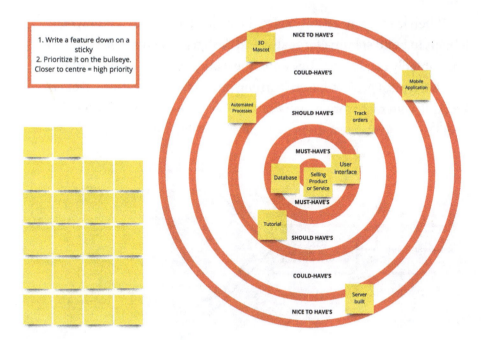

Figure 7-6. *Bullseye visual model and how to apply it when prioritizing features*

Design for Solving Problems Together

PjBL environments support a process where learners develop the capacity to solve real-world problems through proposing prototypes instead of ideas. Problems come in all shapes and sizes and they can be simple, complex, or in the case of an emerging technology project, wicked or ill-structured. Problems are ill-structured because there is no one solution path. These types of problem are common with real-world problems as development teams balance between what is feasible, define problem spaces, prioritize features and the skills team members may or may not have for the tasks required. Solutions are greatly informed by the learners assigned to them, propelled in new directions through client interactions. New solutions can emerge quickly and require students to adapt previously defined solutions—all in large part determined by the design problem the learners must solve.

When learners iteratively solve the zone of unknown unknowns, it helps to build stamina for real-world design problems they will undoubtedly tackle after they enter the workforce. The map in Figure 7-7 shows a typical project-based learning process with a real-world client. Working with real-world clients can up the stakes for learners, build resilience, and connect them to a relevant problem-to-solve.

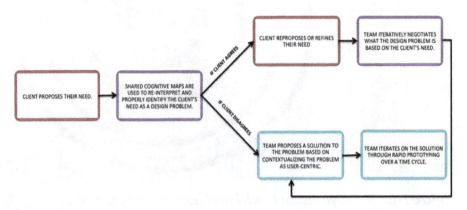

Figure 7-7. *A cyclic process of proposing solutions to clients as prototypes*

Giving your learners a problem to solve together is not really a new disruption in learning environments. Handing them an ill-structured problem to solve through the design of a prototype, on the other hand, has numerous advantages. In the field of study of problem-solving, ill-structured problems demand learners to contend with uncertainty, especially when they are at times "aiming in the dark."

"What is the problem we are trying to solve?"

In solving ill-structured problems, teams learn to apply the best process to solve the problem in the moment and move forward knowing that while the current solution may be optimal at the time, it's never perfect. Prototypes are the perfect vehicle because they offer teams an object that can test whether it solved a particular problem it set out to solve. Learners at times have difficulty identifying the problem properly, and once they settle on what they think is the problem, they have difficulty letting go of all the work that went into co-constructing a prototype that solved the problem they may have mis-identified. This might also be due to not defining the problem space well. At a certain point, it will be important for learners to balance a continual emphasis on solving problems with a focus on proposing solutions, understanding the cycle of proposing solutions as a more generative way to move forward beyond framing their work solely as problem-solving.

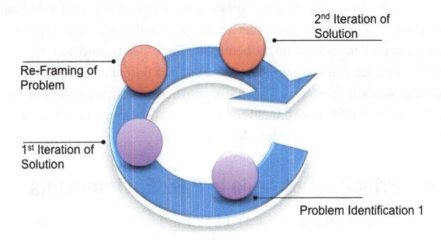

Figure 7-8. *Cycle of identifying a problem then iterating on its solutions*

Design for Agility

Designing for agility has two meanings. The first is to create a design of learning that allows learners to practice being agile in the literal sense of the term, being nimble with the practiced capacity to move quickly and easily. The second refers to Agile with a capital A as a project management methodology that supports individuals and teams in being agile. Many learners undertaking a PjBL course focused on emerging technology co-construction are unfamiliar with Agile as a project management methodology. New to them is that many software development projects orient toward changing requirements that happen when they make iterative attempts to create interactive prototypes that solve a specific design problem. Learners are not familiar with how to manage unpredictable cycles of software development. They are unfamiliar with all the component parts that make it work. They lack the experience to break down their weekly work into short Sprints and review their efforts each time before launching into the next Sprint cycle. They also need to know that ideally, at the completion of each Sprint, they can test how interact with a representation of their final product. They need to learn that prototypes provide all stakeholders with an idea of the functionality that will be integrated within the final product. They also need to understand the benefit of a Retrospective and how the results of the feedback that they receive can inform the continued direction of the project's development. They also would benefit from knowing that they will at first have difficulties timeboxing how much time they "should" spend on their project, but that over time it will get better.

Core Principles of Agile in PjBL Environments

When considering the design of a PjBL course that tasks learners with developing new technology, it's critical to provide practice and reference to some of the core principles of Agile. The Agile Manifesto is a good starting point for those wishing to teach Agile in a learning environment. Many find that Agile is a perfect complement to PjBL environments, particularly with one of its core characteristics of continuous improvement.

Agile is differently applied in a learning environment than in a more established workplace. In the workplace, there may be more defined roles on a team that apply and ensure that the principles of Agile are being followed. It is useful to identify those core principles of Agile and then talk through how they manifest in a PjBL environment.

Agility

The practiced ability to be flexible about changes to what a final project becomes (within some design constraints). Learners will struggle with making changes especially if they become attached to their work. The value of continuous improvement is important to impart when this occurs.

Continuous Improvement

The improvement of a prototype over time in addition to the improvement of individual and team performance is a characteristic that may not be front and center in workplace environments, but it is essential in learning environments. This is because of the inherent feedback that learners expect and how that feedback can improve their offerings as they progress through the course, as signs and assignments that demonstrate improvement will inform your evaluation of their effort.

Velocity

Agile teams are reflective, and through their Retrospectives, they become increasingly aware as to their approach to the project they are developing, including how to increase their efficiency so they can recognize patterns of delivery, remove obstacles, and hopefully fulfill more tasks. This is a constant stress in Agile product development with pros and cons. There does exist a rapid acceleration of all team processes over time once the team becomes increasingly aligned to what they are co-constructing. Conversely, there can also be a deceleration for a variety of reasons. Velocity then becomes a tool to measure progress and the team's trajectory, with constant microadjustments for unforeseen events. Learners can benefit from understanding how well their work flows as they improve their individual performance.

Goal Setting

Individual and team goals are important to aim for even though they may not always get there. There are several methods that can be used including SMART goals that are specific, measurable, achievable, relevant, and time bound. Sprint goals also provide a framework for teams to achieve goals. Students will benefit from practicing Sprint goals to keep them within scope for a single Sprint and keep these goals in mind in the context of how the goals reflect larger milestones in a pipeline. These can be periodically reviewed at the end of each Sprint during Retrospectives to ensure the individual and team is on track to achieve defined goals.

Prioritizing

When students first start to learn about Agile while developing project ideas, they sometimes think they can achieve all of the features that will contribute to a project. This is mainly because they may not truly understand what features go into a project nor how they will be broken down and managed. They don't have the experience of breaking down all features into tasks or estimating how long each task will take to perform. Different prioritization tools can help support the relationship between effort and time across various phases of a production.

The first in ideation can draw attention to larger features that will contribute to the final deliverable. These must-haves are prioritized over nice-to-haves. An example of a must-have for a project that involves some type of password-protected login on a web portal is the need for encryption and in many cases a database. A nice-to-have in this same case might be a dancing 3D avatar that pops out of the user interface and reminds you to choose a password that is hard to crack. Every task that contributes to a feature during a Sprint needs to also be prioritized. Identifying what feature needs to be co-constructed first is always a good question to ask a team of learners so that they start to prioritize the order in which they do things. When teams undertake a Sprint, tasks will surface that teams missed writing out at the beginning of their Sprint. This can happen especially when they are developing something new or something they have never done before, which will lead to unpredictable results.

Those missed tasks or features are revealed when work is undertaken and, if incomplete at the end of a Sprint, end up in the Backlog. The Backlog consists of an itemized list of missed tasks or features that needs to be reviewed and re prioritized for the next Sprint. Critical tasks undertaken to realize core features will affect what the team can achieve over the entire project timeline.

Iterating

Students will take a few weeks or more to learn that activities they engage in with associated artifacts including prototypes all contribute toward a final project they submit at the end of a 12-week semester. Their offerings, especially once in the Production phases of their projects, are versions of what came before, with added or removed features, that result in higher levels of fidelity of their prototype. Every assignment they submit can be iterative if you choose that a feedback cycle is essential. Important to impart is that there will always be the impulse and need to improve work, and that the work they do in the course are iterations that will likely lead to a Proof of Concept. The differences between a Proof of Concept and a Minimum Viable Product will be important to distinguish between as learners will be unfamiliar as to how each type of prototype relates to the projects they are undertaking. Those insights will include a discussion of fidelity, number of features, level of user interaction, purpose, consistency, and debugging, to name a few.

Feedback

Learners need explicit feedback for the prototypes they engage in co-constructing together. They seldom come to the course with the knowledge and experience that guarantees they will be an A student. Students need support structures and Rules of Play to understand the type of feedback they will receive, how to receive it, and in turn how to articulate feedback that will be helpful to others when developing a project together in what is hopefully a safe environment for everyone. Feedback in Agile is built into its cyclic structure which lends well to providing numerous touchpoints within a PjBL learning environment. Feedback they give and receive can occur within facilitated in-class presentations of their work, and in Retrospectives where individuals give each other feedback on the contributions they make to their projects. Retrospectives are important to model and observe. This is because learners are just starting to develop the critical language necessary to support one another in emerging technology development. They will benefit from you as both observer of a Retrospective and mediator if a person's comments are not clear or misunderstood by their team members. Rules of Play around communication may need to be repeated and refined to ensure an equitable and respectful critical environment.

Communication

Agile thrives in offering learners, who take part in a co-construction process, multiple touchpoints where they can continuously improve their communication. This makes it an ideal feature of a PjBL course in that it offers learners with multiple methods and mediums to communicate their ideas, plans, feedback, and contributions. A key tool in Agile is Scrum. Scrum as a daily Agile ritual is an essential communicative principle that Agile proposes, allowing learners to update each other on what they've done, what they will do, and any obstacles they might encounter that the members of the team might be able to help them with. Another communication tool regularly used by teams as a place to share work in progress and receive feedback is Dailies. Since undergraduates in a PjBL course typically are engaged in other courses, however, they are referred to in this case as Weeklies. Weeklies provide an opportunity for learners to practice communicating their ideas in a concise manner and to practice asking for specific feedback that will benefit the current state of their project. While daily communication is difficult for undergraduates in-between classes, you can recommend that learners adopt a work-based social media channel. Finally, at the end of every Sprint, students are offered another opportunity to improve and practice communication, during Retrospectives. Retrospectives, or Retros, allow teams to use a variety of different reflection tools that challenge them to reflect on the work they achieved in their last Sprint. At the end of a Retro, and based on what they learned from it, teams then plan their next Sprint. Some teams make efforts to improve task estimation, communication, and ways that they managed their work in their next Sprint plan.

Agile vs. Agility

As mentioned, there are several meanings of the word agile. When focused on agility in the literal sense, there are many ways to practice it and embed these activities that help learners to practice agility within the PjBL course design. To support how you support learners in practicing agility, it will be helpful to define what agility might mean for you and how agility might be demonstrated when it comes to team performance in the course you design. To do so, first think of what has made you more agile or conversely what has made you less agile. Draw from what you know first and then see if you can transpose it into some type of activity that the students can engage in. The relationship between agility and sports is a good starting point. What are the circumstances that can make a person more agile? How can learners be trained to improve their agility? What is the connection between flow and agility? What about a student's capacity to adapt to change?

Activities that allow learners to practice agility do not necessarily have to be those associated with Agile project development. One example to practice agility in-person is to facilitate a ball passing activity. Teams pass a ball to one another for seven rounds and are given multiple chances to shorten how long it takes to do so. Competing with other teams provokes them to find creative ways to reduce their time. There are more targeted activities to practice agility that directly relate to deepening learner understanding of Agile that you can undertake. This includes the Dream Home activity visualized in Figure 8-9 (Chapter 8).

Daily Scrum

Persistent communication is the hallmark of any Agile pipeline. It's important to stay in touch persistently because you need to give everyone on the team an update as to where you're at with the completion state of the tasks you've taken on. Scrum solves the problem of depending on others and not knowing where they are at. Installing Scrum as a persistent best practice requires supervision and constant reminding. This is because most students are used to working alone. They also are not in the habit of connecting with other students in-between classes. Providing an update on the tasks they are working on, is dependent on when each student undertakes those tasks, and how quickly they complete them. It also speaks to the prioritization of tasks related to the PjBL course in relation to the other courses that learners are taking. Timing and prioritization fluctuate depending on the student. What will benefit mentors and students is in coming up with a due date of completion for tasks that are related to the project deliverables each week. So, if the class is Tuesday, then learners need to be in a state of completion by x day of the week.

Creating a persistent delivery day helps students manage what they are doing in your class with the rest of the classes they also have to take and manage.

Weeklies

When Agile teams present their work to other teams working on different projects, they become open to feedback and may break down any resistance to change they might feel. Project features change and it's a natural part of the process to take a few steps back before moving forward as the process of continuous improvement will lead to a better proof of concept, team dynamic, and cohesion. Feedback needs to be facilitated by a mentor, ensuring that critical feedback is tempered and is informed by a principle of continuous improvement. Feedback received during Weeklies offers teams the possibility of agility. They need to respond, especially if the feedback is so well thought through that ignoring it would not lead to an improved project. That potential to adapt is part of why Agile processes are so good at dealing with the unexpected. Weeklies provide teams the ability to adapt and manage change. Often, through feedback, unforeseen tasks present themselves, in part because initial requirements may not have been completely identified. It's difficult to think of everything that you might need for a project especially if you are creating something new that no one on the team has ever done before. In addition, breaking down all the subtasks required to complete one task is usually underestimated, and the completion of existing tasks may take more time than initially predicted.

Backlogs and Parking Lots

Agility can also mean responding quickly to a changing situation, bouncing back to keep the flow. In an Agile project, sometimes not everyone's idea is followed through on. This is not because of a lack of equity or of being inclusive. It speaks to a previous principle of Agile:

the importance of prioritizing ideas. The equitable principle of Agile is it allows those ideas that were not used to either be implemented later in the current project pipeline (Backlog) or to not be used during this production pipeline but considered for further phases of development (Parking Lot). Both methods are ways to acknowledge everyone's ideas and have their voices heard. Backlogs are the place where tasks or features reside, whereas the Parking Lot contains features that the team has to temporarily abandon. They can also be referred to as ideas that go into an "icebox" for future Sprints or projects—a good idea, but not yet achievable given the time constraints of the current project and the features that have been prioritized. The use of both tools creates a more efficient workflow and allows the team to align on what is essential for the current phase of the project.

Design for Emerging Technologies

Investigations of the learning experience and phenomena related to PjBL environments are not actively implemented in post-secondary. It's even more challenging to locate research that investigates the learning experience of PjBL environments focused on emerging technology development. What is key in understanding is that PjBL environments can appeal to industry and faculty partnerships as learners can create emerging technology prototypes and learn while they are doing so. The results of their work can lead to a variety of different types of research.

Some, focus on the creative process itself that results in some type of unique user-experience, whether a virtual, augmented or mixed reality research creation (for example). Other types of research investigate the phenomena related to what a user experiences. This usually requires an artifact to be co-constructed, followed by research that might investigate comfort factor, how engaging or immersive the experience is, or how the research creation might impact how people learn.

A few examples include conducting experimental studies that leverage technologies like VR to study their effect on empathy and stroke rehabilitation. Research has also been conducted to understand how VR experiences might induce feelings of awe, immersion and connection. The creation of emerging technology that can act as proof of concepts for future research is a valuable reason to facilitate PjBL in post-secondary.

Advantages of Cyclic Development of Emerging Technologies in PjBL

Agile and emerging technologies are well suited to PjBL environments since the co-creation of new technologies will benefit from cycles of development that can be reflected on and improved. Navigating learner activities around the cyclic nature of co-constructing emerging technology prototypes gets them used to their potential transition into communities of practice where different versions of Agile are practiced. What teams learn and how they document what they learn throughout a PjBL pipeline prepare them for companies who are increasingly valuing innovation as part of their long-term strategy.

The cyclic nature of manifesting prototypes through Agile sprints results in multiple advantages for learners. Through cycles of development, learners:

- Identify the prioritized features that contribute to the user experience

- Improve at breaking down a feature into tasks

- Experience the connection between iterative prototyping and the continuous improvement of their efforts over time

- Realize their responsibility for completing tasks that others are depending on in every Sprint

- Learn the value of creating prototypes at various levels of fidelity and resolution

- Review the process of co-construction in daily and weekly cycles with structured reflections

- Become less attached to ideas with the realization that sometimes features not possible to complete may be carried over to the next Sprint or 'parked' for future project phases

- Practice proposing ideas and advocating for ideas that they believe are important to include in a project. They also practice doing so for one another's ideas increasing buy-in, trust, empathy and alignment.

- Increase their practice of communicating their own design process persistently

Choose the x in xR

In choosing an emerging technology to develop within a PjBL environment, it allows for many problems to surface, each a fantastic learning experience for students. The x in xR, refers to any type of medium that augments and extends our shared physical reality. xR projects are laden with development problems. Consistent performance of xR experiences are rare, forcing learners to troubleshoot, debug, reoptimize, and in turn, reconsider the user experience. Situations could include Augmented Reality applications that are too big to launch or whose QR codes don't trigger an animation. It could be a multiplayer VR experience where some people have difficulty logging in and others see nothing on the screen. Challenges persistently surface in mixed-reality experiences that are supposed to offer users a world that merges the physical and virtual one to varying degrees, and yet important dialogue cannot be heard because of too much outside ambient noise. And these are not the only xs in xR. We have no idea what other types of emerging technologies will draw our attention in the future. Regardless of which medium learners develop in a project-based course, emerging technologies propose enough challenges and problems to engage learners to practice their problem-solving skills persistently.

Design for Prototyping

Most learners have misconceptions as to what a prototype is. A PjBL course can reinforce the idea that tangible artifacts, whether real world or virtual, can all be versions of, representations of what will come. This is a key feature of PjBL that manifests time and again. Learners become increasingly motivated by this factor since most of their training tasks them with creating some type of written artifact that must be perfect if their final effort is what is assessed. Prototypes also answer design questions and guide students on what they will build that will best solve a design problem.

In PjBL, learner efforts along the way all contribute to an assessment so they have a better idea of how they are doing with the knowledge they are gaining. Every manifestation of student effort can improve. Mentors provide learners with every opportunity to improve their understanding of the course content through assignments as prototypes. When we design for prototyping, we draw from an established tradition that can offer us a wide variety of tools across disciplines. These include visual models, design thinking tools and strategies, heuristics, different forms of prototypes, testing assumptions, user-testing protocols, etc. Prototypes allow students to express their understanding of a project brief as a tangible artifact, iterate on the problem to solve, test design biases and assumptions, improve their communication process, and create ever-improving prototypes at increasing levels of fidelity. Through prototyping, learners practice developing, managing, and analyzing user tests. They learn to test hypotheses that inform the prototype's iterative development. And at the end of a course, they have a tangible artifact to center their experience of the PjBL environment.

Iteration

When caught up in iterating different versions of their prototypes based on the feedback they receive, students learn the value of listening, of receiving feedback to improve their next offering. They learn that every single offer that they make can be improved upon and this dramatically transforms their educational experience, which they can apply to their other courses and in the work place once they graduate.

Low to High

Integrated within the concept of iterating is that learners will improve the fidelity of their offers each time they engage in recreating it. In other words, the medium or container they are co-constructing will visually, orally, and kinaesthetically improve. There is also an increase of interactivity for users who engage with a more developed prototype with an increasing number of features. As teams shift from lower to higher fidelity prototypes, it's important that each version addresses the design questions that learners ask and what they want to test. For example, if they want to test what characters will most resonate with their target users, they may only need to draw them in 2D vs. taking the time to create 3D characters. Persistently asking students the intent of their current prototype will draw attention to the energy placed in its co-construction, how it will benefit their targeted users, and how they'll know.

Always Incomplete

Prototypes are never perfect representations of an idea that solve some type of human need or problem. Learners embody that value over time by engaging in the practice weekly. That philosophy or value to prototyping lessens the stakes for delivering something that is perfect. It should not sway students, however, to deliver the best possible result from their combined efforts. This may need to be persistently mentioned along the project pipeline. Learners will benefit from regarding prototypes as a combination of effort that gets as close as they can to answering design questions about the eventual final product.

User Testing

We test a prototype to receive feedback from a user—to learn about whether it answers a design question when a user interacts with it. At the end of each Agile Sprint, whatever prototypical state the prototype is in, students will benefit from one or more aspects of it being tested. Testing can focus on how well a user understands what to do when presented with a user interface. Students will benefit from being taught to have a research purpose for their user test, develop questions for users to respond to after a user test, and define the methods of analyzing user responses to help them decide how to improve features of the prototype for the next test. When user tests are conducted by teams, there are multiple roles that can also be defined. Learners need to know this. So, while the product is being tested, the development team can be guided to take notes through observation or ask targeted questions of the users. A clearly organized user test will allow for more useful data to be used by the team to inform continued development.

Design for (Re)learning the Value of Productive Failure

It's not often that we get the chance as designers to rework our creations over a long period of time. We are usually constrained by timelines, the influence of the visioneer, etc. I was fortunate to have that rare opportunity to work on a show that was remounted three times over the course of a five-year period. Like any sound design process, time doesn't always allow for you to be perfectly satisfied with all the compositions that contribute to an overall show. In the show I was working on, there was this one cue that I just wasn't happy with. The feeling with the director was mutual. On the first production, I created no less than twelve iterations of this one damn cue that I just couldn't get right. I had another opportunity with the next remount a few years after, but after another dozen versions, the director and I shook our heads with a "no that's not quite the right fit" either. We tried different tracks. We tried silence. We tried sfx. We tried live voices or just going with the sound of books dropping from the grid, which was a part of how the scene played out. But to no avail. A few years passed and I received a phone call that once again, I had the opportunity to rework the sound design. At the top of the list was the dreaded library cue. To me it felt like the last opportunity I might have to get that damn cue right. In rehearsals, I tried at least two dozen new tracks, and again, nothing worked. So, after five years and over two dozen iterations, I decided to take an opposite approach that I had learned from a few other shows I had designed sound for over the years. I wrote what I thought was an inappropriate cue that in my head I knew would never work and brought it into tech—that part of a theater production where all the design elements are rehearsed with actors in the actual theater. It was time to try the library cue: SQ 32.5. I played the track hesitantly, and for some strange and fascinating reason, it worked. The director looked at me

*and I at her and our jaws dropped in perfect synchronicity.
The persistence to iterate until getting it right, until it's right
for the show, to not be precious about what you write, and to
keep trying, were all big lessons learned. And believe me, many
of the failed attempts for that scene I would come to use in at
least ten other productions over the years. There were no failed
impulses. The time and place for that track with that scene
came together in that moment and the show went on.*

The only problem with failure is our association with the word. And
when working on emerging technology projects, it would benefit you and
your students to express associations with the word, then deprogram your
associations with it, and reinvent its use as a valuable tool for continuously
improving our efforts over time. Most people will tell you that failure is the
opposite of winning, but a new breed of success stories coming from the
world of software development reveals that it's complementary. Think of
how Slack as a social communication platform was originally intended as
an internal tool for a game development team. Perhaps the team failed to
release their video game, but in the process created a robust communication
application that dominated the office-based messaging market.

Unplanned success stories aside, students who are just starting to get
an idea of what they are good at need a little compassion and empathy
when it comes to understanding how much they want to succeed. In our
school systems, to fail is not to pass. It is the worst fear of anyone who
has lived through a statistics or physics class, or any student forced to
take a final exam that informs whether or not they can continue down an
educational path based on their ability to memorize knowledge or apply
memorized mathematical formulas.

*"You're not going to get into math or science are you?", professor
Rodney asked me when I went in to see final exam results in my
last year of high school. "Nope," I replied. "I'm going to be a musi-
cian." "Congratulations, then," he said. "You got a 51 in Calculus."*

In PjBL environments, your learners will constantly fail, at least on their first attempts to fulfill an activity or assignment related to human-centered design. It is built into the design especially because most students are just starting to learn about how to navigate their intelligence in unknown territory. Anticipate that many students will not "get it" on their first attempts, and plan to give them more chances to succeed. Allowing learners to iterate on assignments permits them to reflect on why they might have not included a part of the assignment that would have resulted in a good assessment. No matter what criteria inform your rubrics for an assignment, it might take them a few tries to understand what a 5 out of 5 means when it comes to "quality of an offer." To give them another opportunity is also a test of their resilience, their capacity to take feedback, respond to it, and improve their second or third or fourth offering. Many learning environments have equated high grades and success with a student's capacity to memorize knowledge, and this is not the case in PjBL. As you develop criteria, you will want to think about different ways to measure how much or what a person learns. In PjBL how well someone learns needs to be reinvented as to how well they can apply a principle you teach to the co-construction of a prototype that solves a human problem.

To Do: Setting Learners Up to Fail

You can set learners up to fail to reinvent their ideas of failure and do so safely without creating anxiety in the process.

- Set up an environment where you state that one Rule of Play today is to fail.

- Set teams of 4 to solving one of the world's most difficult problems (environment, energy, etc.).

- Give them a difficult time constraint (ten minutes) to come up with a solution.

- Regardless of how amazing the result is, ensure that one or more part of their idea that they pitch to everyone fails.

- Facilitate a debrief session where you ask learners how they felt about failing.

- Tell them they have another ten minutes to come up with a different solution.

- No matter what their result, reward them for their efforts not for the solution they provide.

No teams are perfect and providing learners with enough leeway to "fail" at certain parts in the production pipeline is strategic. Knowing this can support your efforts to design activities that can target a particular part of the pipeline that you know will be a challenge for students to understand without experiencing it a few times. For example, you can integrate in your design "forced" failure points through strategic questions or tasks in any given Sprint. A strategy some mentors have used in previously conducted research was to allow students to over scope work in an early Sprint in order for them to have the lived experience of over scoping. Having learners report on progress each week during Weeklies will help reinforce the message of needing to be more judicious with how time is spent, particularly given all the other courses your learners are likely taking.

Identifying challenges over time and developing a system to resolve them is one of the skills that individuals and teams develop as practitioners. Developing new ideas with emerging technologies affords team members the lived experience of making mistakes, and realizing that the important part of the mistake-making process is developing a process to resolve them and the resilience to keep going regardless. Some of the ways learners fail quickly in development projects include

- Alignment on project source file organization

- Rapid analysis and then integration of user-testing data beyond internal team tests

- Disorganized meeting structures or no structures at all

- Imbalanced workloads

- Not always knowing what other team members are doing in a Sprint

- Not always sure what to do themselves when they complete their tasks

- Understanding what needs to be decided upon in the ideation phase prior to starting production

- Being incapable of moving forward as they want 100% clear requirements before proceeding

- Not integrating client partner feedback into their very next prototype

- Incapable of evening out task distribution

- Poor communication to client partners in terms of project status updates

- Poor understanding of dependencies

- Trouble or resistance asking for help

- Problems responding to team members, client partners or the instructor quickly, or when it really matters

When you start to consider all the complexities inherent in an emerging technology production pipeline, you can also see how many opportunities there are for learners to improve their failure productively. Areas of improvement can directly relate to criteria that inform your assessment of them.

Design for Collaboration
Agile Alignment

Because of the persistently changing nature of designing prototypes in Agile learning environments, there is a necessity for student teams to remain persistently aligned. They are not used to having to do this. A lot of classes in post-secondary leave the progress of a student for them to deal with. Depending on your team members, to contribute to the success of a project that informs the assessment of that project is a feature of PjBL that is not commonly experienced in other types of courses. Often, we hear of silos in the workplace, and it is a similar challenge in academic ones. Many individuals have difficulty zooming out and seeing the big picture, and understanding their role in the execution of a project. Therefore, it will benefit students to understand why alignment is fundamental for collaborating well with others. Once the reasoning is clear, then tools can be introduced.

A lack of alignment is one reason why the implementation of a daily Scrum ritual is an important tool for you to teach and then mentor teams on using properly. Scrum rituals across different types of disciplines and projects tend to also be customized. The process can be structured in such a way as to allow student-team members to realize the value of knowing what task their team members are engaged in completing, if they are struggling with a task, and their progress in completing a task. It connects them in-between classes and keeps their project a priority through the dizzying number of other courses and related assignments they have to simultaneously undertake. When it comes to reporting blockers or obstacles, it's common for learners to talk about not having enough time to deliver what they said they would. Anticipate this, particularly midsemester when some learners will have to prioritize their midterm exams in other courses. It can be highly stressful. Some solutions include planning a course timeline where midsemester activities can consist of Retrospective activities for the class and the beginning of a new cycle or phase of work. Another is to ensure learners persistently deliver on what they've promised to deliver any given week after the sixth class.

By encouraging persistent communication and an intentional reorganization of priorities, while balancing out their other courses, learners can better understand the big picture of how the course fits into their own prioritization matrix. When scoping their projects, they need to reflect on their own capacities and make reasonable and negotiated commitments. While it is difficult at first to have a sense of just how big a scope students can be reasonably expected to take on, it is important to do so, as you are teaching them good habits that they can bring to the workplace. Teaching them to look ahead will teach team members to rely on one another and improve how they plan task completion in relationship to the dependencies they have on one another. They will also benefit from any time management strategies you have to share that can help them maintain a healthy work habit.

Learners will also benefit and align on how important each of their roles are, if you underline the idea of dependencies on a bigger-picture scale. For example, in order for the team to create a vertical slice of one level of a side-scrolling video game, an overall design has to be in place, and art assets for character, UI, and environment need to be developed and these have to be programmed to interact with each other and the user within a specific software development environment. Without art, there can only exist a low-fidelity prototype that demonstrates a game mechanic. Without programming, the highest fidelity 3D model cannot be placed in an environment that demonstrates the game mechanics. Without a design, the user will have no idea of the rules of the game, nor what to do. The more aligned learners are on how the tasks they contribute to the overall final prototype they will deliver, the better the result will be.

Making Ideas Visible

The use of visual maps to share ideas visibly with team members has been gaining widespread acceptance in small, medium, and large enterprises with an eye toward creating innovative products and the "next big thing." Visual maps have been a part of the design process for many years. One of the first documented is a distribution channel map created by the Walt Disney Company. This map illustrates the various ways in which the Walt Disney Company can reach its intended target consumer, through their movies, through Disneyworld, products, etc. While mind mapping and concept mapping seem to have received most of the attention in professional and academic writing, there are many more kinds of maps with specific purposes that have not been written about. Each of these is incredibly useful in PjBL courses. The facilitation of visual models seems to fall into the category of design or design processes and is associated within the fields of service design thinking, design thinking, strategic design, value proposition design, and others. Companies like Ideo have thrived in this area, offering visual models as one solution to the complex and difficult-to-navigate world of the design process.

Persistent alignment along the production pipeline is one of many reasons that design thinkers often use to discuss the positive advantages of using visual maps to represent, capture, and organize their ideas visibly. There are many champions of this process since visual models are highly adaptive to in-the-moment team needs, effective in capturing ideas succinctly, quickly focus students to a shared visual representation of a problem to solve, and appeal to visual learners, adding a change of rhythm and variety to how students are used to learning.

Think of the types of visual maps or models you've used in your professional career and see how their use can be plotted throughout a development pipeline. There are many resources dedicated to improving visual fluency. The Periodic Table of Visualization Methods comes to mind as a good resource to experience a wide variety of visual models. Common ones that have been used PjBL courses at the Master of Digital Media Program include the following:

- Variations on mind mapping using a central idea with nodes shooting from it that form part of that idea. These include many types of initial brainstorming with examples like Rules of Play for team, identifying Core Values a team wants to have, initial Feature Storm. Using an image at the center of a mind map is also common with the *Persona* visual model (Figure 7-4).

- *Storyboards* can help teams deconstruct any aspect of the user experience, customer journey, and can help them keep the human experience top of mind when prototyping (Figure 7-5).

- Landscape models such as the *What IF* map that help students brainstorm and scope blue-sky ideas (Figure 7-3).

- Visual metaphor visual models like the *bullseye* visual model that helps teams prioritize features among other things (Figure 7-6).

Culture Tools

One of the most underestimated aspect of any team engaged in production pipelines is directing their attention to building and sustaining a team culture. This is as true in the workplace as it is in post-secondary project-based courses. What is a good team culture to have? How have you cultivated or contributed to the one that you were part of? What are the essential characteristics of a good team culture? You can probably agree that it doesn't just magically happen on its own without a lot of effort. As a mentor, you can help provide tools and approaches to learners to develop their own team culture. These include some of the tools already discussed such as facilitating teams to define their *Core Values* and developing *Rules of Play (Appendix 1)*. But that's just the beginning. For a team culture to be maintained, students will need persistent reminders to check in and reflect on the health of their team culture. These can be facilitated in class.

Persistent reference to the importance of maintaining team culture is important as it might not be obvious for teams to take the time to do so. For example, suggesting a team goes to eat lunch together and bond over food is always a great way to break the ice. If the team is remote, then virtual coffees and games can be an effective way to spend time together away from the routine of fulfilling tasks solely related to project development. On the other hand, related activities to the project can accomplish two things at the same time. For example, learners gather to play card games if their project tasks them to design their own. If they are designing a remote escape room game, then they will benefit from going out and experiencing one on their own. If, as in Figure 7-9, they are designing a couch-based iPad game for four based on Sumo wrestlers, then it will pay off in the long run for them to experience the sport through video, watching it live, or actually playing it.

Figure 7-9. *Physically prototyping an iPad Sumo game at the MDM Program*

Design for Adapting to Change

When you teach a project-based course, you will quickly notice the need to adapt what it is you are teaching every week. By modelling your capacity to adapt, students also learn how important adaptability is when developing emerging technologies. Adapting what you teach, and your mentoring style and strategies, is the realistic nature of being in a creative and agile space with all types of learners from different disciplinary backgrounds who have varying degrees of the following:

- Experience working with other people.

- Experience with social constructivist-oriented courses like PjBL.

- Experience developing technology alone or on teams.

- Varying levels of skills in specific knowledge areas that require associated tasks to be performed.

- Various levels of commitment to a course when other courses may also need to be taken simultaneously.

- Different capacities to listen and then act on the feedback they receive from you and the rest of the class.

- How much they need to be retrained to self-regulate when the dominant mode of teaching has been to be regulated by teachers before your class.

- Their fluency experience with a variety of digital media technologies.

One of the most important takeaways learners can have from a PjBL course is that their resilience to adapt to change will improve. Changing features, changing their idea of success, refining their assignments iteratively, receiving feedback on a prototype that demands change, letting go of their "*precious*," and pivoting should all be encouraged.

Design for Reflection

An essential core feature of the overall learning design is persistent reflection. Time for individual, team, and class reflection should be always considered throughout every part of your course. This is what makes teaching and mentoring in a learning environment so different than in the workplace. We can and should afford the time to do so and, when necessary, guide the reflection, using Socratic questioning as a method to elicit reflection. Reflective practices will manifest as

- Persistent and guided group reflection in every class on the tools being used, processes being facilitated, and projects being presented

- Guidelines for learner propositions at every stage of the collaborative process

- Individual self-assessment on collaborative ability in week 6 or 7 of the course

- A minimum of three Sprint Retrospectives for teams during the entire semester

- A final facilitated group assessment of the materials they learned, what might improve the course moving forward

Retrospectives are a form of documented inquiry into the software development process or pipeline itself. The implementation of specific Retrospective tools during the Agile process can generate some useful information that can support teams in identifying problems, improving their approach to solving them in subsequent development cycles. Retrospective tools offer teams working in Agile production environments the opportunity to reflect on how they individually and as a group managed the co-construction of features that led to testable prototypes. For practitioner/researchers, documented Retrospectives can also serve as data that when analyzed can provide teams with an understanding of common themes, especially when Retrospective data is collected and analyzed cyclically.

Persistent Feedback

As a mentor, if you don't preplan feedback milestones in your design of learning, you will constantly be asked to provide weekly feedback to a small percentage of learners who actively seek it. You can change this interaction pattern by formalizing the process of giving and receiving feedback throughout the course. Persistent feedback can be integrated into comments on assignments, showing exemplar assignments in the class and why they have been chosen to show everyone, and midterm team peer review that is facilitated using a specific feedback visual model. The important thing to remember is that once learners see the value of feedback beyond just "How can I get an A in this course?", then they will see it as a valuable method for them to improve what they are learning in your course.

One of the goals of your mentoring is to get learners to that place. Grades are important for learners as they impact progress in the fulfillment of their degree and, in some cases, help maintain or secure scholarships. Just as important, however, is the cognitive link students make between an assessment they receive, and the degree to which they have embodied tools that will prepare them to transition to digital media communities of practice. In some PjBL courses taught at the graduate level, tasking learners to include a self-assessment grade along with a written explanation as to why they would grade themselves in that way can demonstrate how self-aware they are and the accuracy of that assessment. Their self-assessment can also inform a small percentage of the final project rubric, its accuracy weighed against your own assessment, the assessment of a client partner, and any peer review assessment contributing to a final grade.

To Do: Targeted Reflection Questions

Facilitating reflection for learners and encouraging them to reflect is an important feature of PjBL. That said, it's just as important to take the time to reflect on your own teaching. Doing so will improve the overall learner experience. You can answer the reflective questions in Figure 7-10, or develop your own.

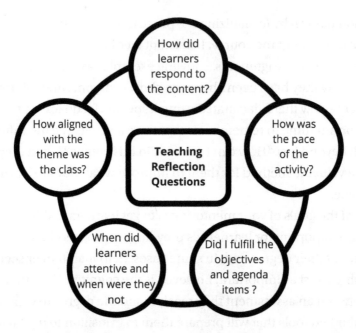

Figure 7-10. Some questions to guide reflection after teaching

Chapter Summary

The knowledge of your own mentoring strategies and how you can apply them to support the core features of a project-based course in emerging technology have prepared you to design week-by-week interactions with learners in a project-based course.

This chapter

- Detailed the core features of a PjBL environment that align with what learners need to know and knowledge areas where they will require mentoring

- Included specific visual models to enhance the teaching of those core features

- Suggested that core features are common to emerging technology development pipelines

- Proposed reflective questions that will help you to improve the overall learner experience in your course

Tools and Suggested Processes

- Designing for creativity using visual models such as the Bad Ideas and What IF brainstorms

- Designing for humans using psychographic models, storyboarding, user stories, and bullseye models to prioritize features that address user needs

- Designing for solving problems iteratively using a variety of approaches including the five Whys visual model

- Designing for agility, prototyping, and emerging technologies to reinforce flexibility, adapt projects based on user testing, and explore innovation with what has yet to be done

- Designing for re(learning) what failure is and designing for supporting learners to improve their capacity to collaborate

- Designing for adapting to change and reflection

- Reflective questions to improve learner UX

Deeper Dive

Babb, J., Hoda, R., & Norbjerg, J. (2014). Embedding reflection and learning into agile software development. *IEEE software*, *31*(4), 51-57.

Vogler, J. S., Thompson, P., Davis, D. W., Mayfield, B. E., Finley, P. M., & Yasseri, D. (2018). The hard work of soft skills: augmenting the project-based learning experience with interdisciplinary teamwork. *Instructional Science, 46*(3), 457-488.

Resource

www.visual-literacy.org/periodic_table/periodic_table.html

CHAPTER 8

Know the PjBL Development Pipeline

Chapter Goal: The goal of this chapter is to offer a model of a typical PjBL course that will help you break down teaching and mentoring activities across a development pipeline.

To apply teaching interventions and mentoring strategies in a PjBL course

You need to understand and design a 12-week course pipeline

So you can iterate on what you teach, in what order, and when you'll need to mentor.

If you are embedded in the digital media industry, then you are most likely very familiar with a technology development pipeline. How might this compare to a similar PjBL pipeline? This chapter will break down an emerging technology pipeline in relation to a typical 12-week 3-credit course at the undergraduate level. Doing so identifies what learners need to be taught along the pipeline and where and when they will need mentoring.

Breaking down an emerging tech pipeline will reveal teaching and learning interaction points you have identified in previous chapters. While there are some processes that may be established across many production pipelines, all projects, and the pipelines they are created within, are unique. That includes the terminology that is used to describe aspects of a

© Patrick Parra Pennefather 2022
P. Parra Pennefather, *Mentoring Digital Media Projects*,
https://doi.org/10.1007/978-1-4842-8798-9_8

pipeline. Learners might have heard of the word prototype, and be able to define what it is, but they don't know the role that prototyping plays in the big picture context of a technology-oriented project pipeline. They likely understand the concept of iterative design but have never gathered the related know-how that accompanies cyclic design patterns when you work with others on a technology development project.

In previous chapters, learner interaction points were identified. What students need to learn needs to be positioned over the course of a 12-week project. In addition, when and how learners will need mentoring can also be plotted over time. Mapping out of what students need to learn and when over a specified time will contribute to your instructional design. What you think students need to learn will also inform the learning outcomes you come to identify. Lastly, visualizing the entire process will help you better understand how much time this will take from your other professional work.

Applying Real-World Development Pipelines to a PjBL One

There are advantages to having managed or having been a part of any emerging technology development pipeline. While each might be different, there is an adaptive structure that can help inform how you mentor a team over time. This is particularly relevant if you've been part of an Agile project pipeline (see Chapter 8). Examining a "typical" Agile-based project management pipeline in Figure 8-1, you'll immediately notice a cyclic component as you move forward in the design (left to right). When you apply this pipeline to a typical 12-week course in a college or university course, you can quickly discern how little time the students will have to accomplish a larger-scale project (see Figure 8-5). That's not to say they shouldn't try to though. What's difficult to measure is how much time teams of individuals are investing in between classes. The expectation is usually 6-8 hours of work on top of class time per week.

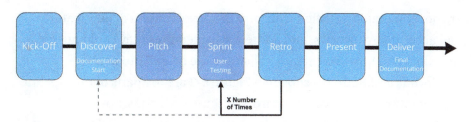

Figure 8-1. *Primary milestones for a project-based course focused on emerging technology*

Kickoff in PjBL refers to the first meeting with learners who interact with the course description, what they'll learn, an introduction to projects, your mentoring style, and a brief or description for each project. This is week 1 where you'll also need to talk through the course outline, explain what the course is about, define your roles, etc.

In Discovery, the team starts to untangle meaning from a one- or two-page Brief; they begin to wrap their heads around what is being asked of them that there may actually be a problem the project will solve. They learn quickly that they'll need to define their Core Values as a collaborating team and in turn identify Rules of Play that will inform dos and don'ts regarding team culture. The Rules of Play visual model functions much like a mind map where learners brainstorm the Rules of Play that will inform their behaviors and performance on the project team they belong to. They may use an assortment of tools to brainstorm ideas and form some sense of a project. Those tools are in many cases up to the mentor to offer and model their use through the in-class teaching session.

Learners will hopefully come out of Discovery understanding the overall project direction and be able to make propositions. Those propositions or pitches are important to share with the rest of the class. Other teams will learn from one another, and all will be able to provide facilitated feedback that the teacher/mentor will facilitate. A Sprint cycle integrates Retrospectives and allows students to review their work and plan a subsequent Sprint based on a new goal, the revision of features they are not completely satisfied with, and the development of new features and accompanying tasks, and address what features they could not get to (Backlog) and how critical they still are to the overall project.

Sprints and Retros as shown in Figure 8-2 are the parts of the pipeline that mainly repeat moving forward. On some occasions, however, if students have completely gone down the wrong track or a client changes their mind, they may have to return to a Discovery phase and begin again. This will result in a project with less features and smaller scope.

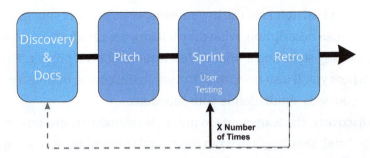

Figure 8-2. *Detail of primary milestones showing cyclic patterns*

Sprints, Scrum, features, tasks, Backlogs, and Retrospectives all form part of one type of Agile methodology whose components all need to be taught. Variations and extensions of Agile have also emerged such as Kanban and Lean and these are worthwhile teaching to students as they may encounter them when they transition into communities of practice that use them. Explaining why some certifications have led to rigidity in applying Agile is also useful for students to know. The best way to do so is to introduce them when students have made their first set of propositions. The cyclic period of Sprints followed by Retrospectives should form the bulk of the course design. Scaled prototyping during Sprints will also need to be facilitated, and in-class teaching time should be partly devoted to a weekly demonstration of different types of paper, physical, interactive, and Wizard of Oz (see Glossary) prototypes from low to high fidelity.

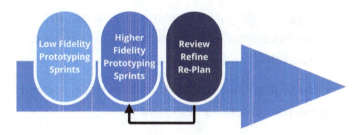

Figure 8-3. *Cyclic pattern involving the development and review of prototypes at different levels of fidelity*

Final team projects should be presented formally. If clients are involved, then they too should attend the presentation. Some tips a week beforehand will help learners include specific parts to their presentation under a mentor's guidance. A rubric for the presentation of the project and another for the final project or deliverable can also be designed.

Designing What Students Need to Learn from a PjBL Experience

What does a typical week-by-week breakdown of a project in a learning environment look like and what needs to be taught? Before diving into *"the what,"* it's important to understand that the development of emerging technologies in a learning environment resonates well to an Agile approach. Following the Agile Manifesto, a relatable and relevant aspect of Agile project development in any learning environment is continuous improvement, which aligns well with PjBL learning outcomes. The pace at which an Agile classroom can move from activity to assignment to activity will be influenced by the learners and their capacity to grasp the following:

- The language of digital co-construction along with use cases and examples so learners begin to understand what is involved and what is possible

- Understanding what's required of them during every phase of the co-construction process

- The assurance that they are moving forward with a project with clear roles, tasks to complete, and clarity on what they will aim for, for a final project deliverable

- Some type of metrics or qualitative understanding that they understand what you are teaching them

- Their work to create a sustainable and communicative team culture in-between set class times in which they support one another

- The adoption of remote work social and communication channels as they will most likely struggle with conflicting schedules quite a bit in-between classes

Teaching and Mentoring Snapshot in a Typical PjBL Course

Figure 8-4 is a snapshot of an iterative approach to designing learning interactions you might engage in when teaching a PjBL course.

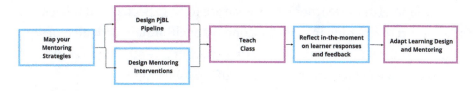

Figure 8-4. *The process of planning your mentoring and teaching strategies in a PjBL course*

Mapping your mentoring strategies will help you identify and articulate the approach to guiding learners through a PjBL course pipeline. That will influence your design and help you plan ahead as to the type of mentoring interactions you can anticipate and plan for. Planning as much as you can will help you stick to some important learning milestones you want to accomplish in the course. That said, once you teach, you will need to reflect in-the-moment and in-between classes, then review your course design, and make adjustments in order to adapt to the rate at which learners are assimilating course content.

In the beginning, the tendency is to overplan too many activities within one class. That impulse is likely motivated by assuming that learners will need a lot of background and prep to be able to jump in quickly and start co-constructing their projects. Knowing this before you even begin your facilitation of the course will help to design course content that can accelerate student understanding of the prototyping process. Also, bear in mind that not all learners will understand the process of developing a project at the same pace. You don't have to move at the pace of those learners who may need more time to digest content and process. It's better to encourage learners to prototype as quickly as you think they can as they will gain a better understanding through doing than through overthinking an iterative process. Supporting learners to create multiple types of prototypes that respond to design questions that may need to be answered and guiding them as to the level of fidelity required to answer those questions will increase their understanding of the role of prototyping in the co-construction process.

Variations in the learner experience are to be expected and reflects the context of teaching in a post-secondary environment with all types of learners from different disciplinary backgrounds enrolling in a PjBL course. Each will have varying degrees of the following:

- Experience working with other people

- Experience with social constructivist-oriented courses like PjBL

- Experience developing technology

- Varying levels of skills in specific knowledge areas that require associated tasks to be performed

- Various levels of commitment to a course when other courses may also need to be taken simultaneously

- Different capacities to listen and then act on the feedback they receive from you and their peers

- How much they need to be retrained to self-regulate when the dominant mode of teaching has been that learners are regulated by teachers before they have come to experience your class

- Their fluency with digital media technologies

- Highly attuned critical mindsets that have been trained to value thinking over doing

Understanding the cyclic nature of what you teach and the necessary repetition of some content that will likely have to occur based on learner responses, will inform the scope of what you teach in the PjBL course you design. As discussed, it's not a bad thing to overscope course content. At first, be ambitious with all you think needs to be taught, but also keep in mind that many learners will require repetition. Avoid rushing through key design features of the course they need to really understand a project pipeline. Keep in mind that it might benefit you to allow for repetition of content as learners transition from Discovery to Production. Many learners get caught up and a bit anxious once they begin prototyping in the Production phase of the class that they can forget about the important aspects of maintaining a communicative and collaborative team culture.

Plotting What You Think Needs to Be Taught in a PjBL Course

In terms of what to teach, you've already broken down all the things you believe are important to teach about an emerging project development cycle. The next step is to look at a typical 12-week course structure and then plot what order content needs to be taught in. Figure 8-5 is one version, which has been taught to student teams to deliver a final minimum viable prototype by the end of a 12-week cycle.

Bear in mind that Figure 8-5 is a template only.

It needs modification based on the particular development pipeline you are familiar with. You've already identified what you think needs to be taught based on your own professional experience in the specific types of productions you've lived through. You may also have a type of technology you want students to learn and targeted who it might be for. For example, you may want your class to focus on technologies for an emerging technology course you've been asked to design in the field of Journalism, Law, Medicine, or Geography. You may have been asked by a specific department to build an emerging technology course. Whatever the discipline, following an iterative project development pipeline will benefit learners and support them in the co-construction process.

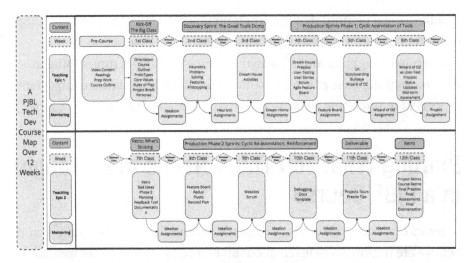

Figure 8-5. *A version of an undergraduate 3-credit PjBL course over 12-13 weeks*

Figure 8-5 is an example of a typical PjBL undergraduate course with 3 in-class hours per week and 6-8 hours in-between weekly classes, that learners are anticipated to engage in completing assignments that all lead toward a minimum viable emerging technology prototype. Content is modified as the course progresses depending on how learners are managing what they need to learn individually, as a team, and as a class. Here is a week-by-week summary:

Precourse content can be made available three weeks prior to the first class. Content includes a reading and videos to prepare them to understand the course as a whole and emphasize that it is a collaborative course that will be focused on co-constructing projects with others.

Week-by-Week Breakdown

Week 1 is orientation week. It's important to walk students through the course outline and the entire learning pipeline. New language needs to be introduced. Your role as both teacher and mentor needs to be defined.

Giving learners an example of what they'll learn would be a good idea. An intro to the idea of a prototype is important to give them an idea of what the final project might look like. Project briefs are discussed so that learners can prepare questions for client partners that should be present in the next class.

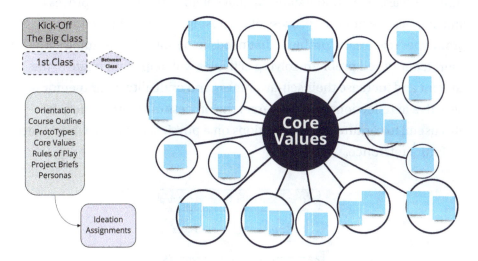

Figure 8-6. *Class 1 with Core Values as sample activity*

Finally, going through a few interactive activities including visual models like the Core Values model will get them familiar with brainstorming and set up some tools to build team culture. You will dominantly teach in this class; however, memorable stories on your professional experience building team cultures will help reinforce its importance. An important assignment is for learners to choose which project they are most interested in co-constructing from a list you have prepared. This will prepare them for the next class in which they will have kickoff meetings with the client partners that you secure.

Week 2 is focused on bringing attention to how individuals and teams solve problems. It frames the motivation of prototypes around the importance of solving human problems. This is not to say there are other types of motivations. Integrating the problem-solving process within the curriculum, however, provides increased opportunities for learners to become more aware of how they resolve team and client problems that collaboration brings to the surface. Relating the iterative attempt at solving problems with prototyping is another key instruction that supports learners in understanding that solving problems is a process and at times the iterative process of proposing solutions in the form of prototypes reveals the problem that needs to be solved. Designing some short team-based problem-solving activities will help them relate to the content and increase their self-awareness and criticality. Your mentor will be active in reflections that can target the process of self-reflection. It is also useful to capture those reflections on a physical or digital whiteboard for future reference.

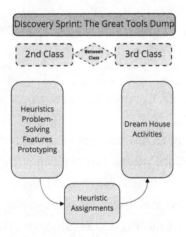

Figure 8-7. *Class 2 and 3 overview*

If you are working with client partners, this is a good time to go over Project Briefs and Q&A with the client partners in attendance. Preparing students with some structured methods that guide them how to undertake a project along with tools that can be applied is valuable. Kick-off meetings with clients provide learners with the experience of building rapport.

It's important for you to be present at initial client meetings to mediate scope when necessary and to provide post-meeting feedback to learners afterwards. To provide them feedback and to mediate scope whenever necessary.

Being present for each team and client meeting will also help to manage the relationship building between client partner and team. An important assignment is to give learners a paper prototyping exercise that they achieve individually. This paper prototype could somehow relate to a group assignment that you design for the next class.

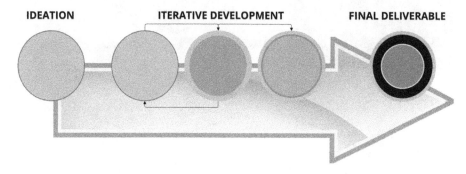

Figure 8-8. *The cyclic nature of iterative development toward a final deliverable*

Week 3 reveals a method for learners to manage their prototypes over time. It does so by condensing the creation of a collaborative project within one class guiding learners through various types of prototypes using an Agile project management structure. This leads to their first collaborative assignment, which is to co-construct a dream home. There are many ways to facilitate the Dream Home activity. Important is to create several iterations of a dream home including paper, physical, and digital as a condensed method to teach Agile. The Dream Home is focused on teaching learners to manage their prototypes in combination with Retrospectives in a short period of time.

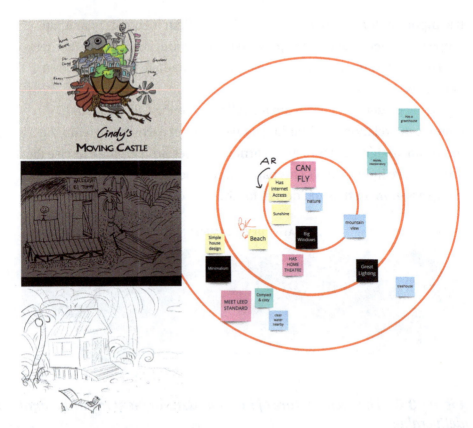

Figure 8-9. *Example of Dream House initial paper prototypes and a bullseye of features*

Week 4 is the first time that learners present their collaborative prototypes. In this class, it's important to guide them through a feedback session and provide some structure to ensure that feedback is constructive and highly participatory. Using the Dream Home activity or any other activity you devise as a use case, can provide learners with a condensed and in-depth analysis of features that contribute to an Agile Feature Board (Appendix 1) and Scrum Board (Appendix 1). In this class, the importance is to relate prototyping to an Agile project management methodology. Assignments are now directly related to unravelling features for their larger projects using the tools you taught in this class. In addition, teaching them Scrum will be of value as a structural meeting tool that you can test every week in class moving forward in the course.

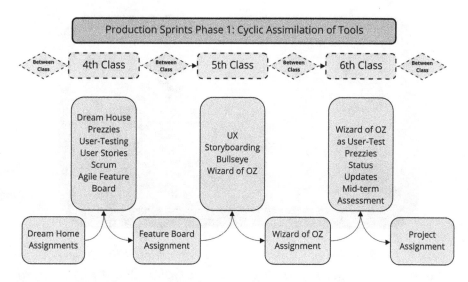

Figure 8-10. *Class 4-6 detail*

Week 5 is focused on feedback with all teams on their identified features and tasks, team roles and responsibilities in relation to task completion, storyboarding their user experiences, and modelling a Wizard of Oz prototype to prepare them for their assignment. Facilitating teams to Scrum in this class is important as is your witnessing of how they do so. This is where your mentor will kick in a little more as you can witness their Scrum and, when necessary, freeze the Scrum and give feedback to support them in their plans.

Week 6 is focused on the dramatization of their Wizard of Oz prototypes. It is recommended that learners are given an opportunity to rapidly change their WOZ prototypes after a round of feedback as the confusion with Wizard of Oz prototypes tends to be centered around demoing features they will build out vs. showing how a user will interact with those features. Students will benefit from furthering their understanding of user-testing. Presenting their WOZ prototypes as user-tests will continue to reinforce the importance of testing prototypes.

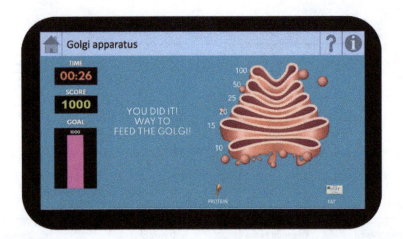

Figure 8-11. *Wizard of Oz prototype co-constructed in powerpoint and demo'd by students learning about the Golgi. One student played the user and the other triggered different features on powerpoint to demonstrate gameplay (with permission from UBC's BioMedical Visualization Certificate program)*

The remainder of the class can be reserved for learners to plan their next Sprints with their teams. If you plan to witness how learners use Scrum, you can also freeze the process and give feedback to support them in the execution of Scrum. This class is a critical halfway point for learners, and by this time, they should have been introduced to prototyping, Agile, and team alignment tools and understood the role of problem-solving with their teams. An important assignment will be for learners to come to the next class with a proposition as to what their final prototype might look like. Lastly, as learners are halfway through a production pipeline and have had enough time with one another, give them a template for a Retrospective so they can submit that as an assignment. The other assignment is a reading that will provoke and inspire learners to consider a pivot (see "Why bad ideas are a good Idea").

Week 7 is the halfway point for learners, and by this class, they should be presenting what the final prototype of their final project might look like. Peer review is important to facilitate and capture so that the entire class can practice giving and receiving offers. Scrum should be integrated in this and every class moving forward to imprint scrum as part of their communication process. Inviting client partners back is also a good idea so they can also add to the feedback cycle and understand where learners are in the development of their projects.

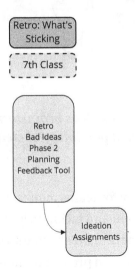

Figure 8-12. Class 7, the midway point

Providing feedback on their Retrospective instrument assignment is also helpful and you can look at the types of things that have been said and most likely elicit more from a team. It's helpful to look at the assigned Retrospective instrument ahead of time if you need to preplan some of what you'll say and to delete any comments that a team would prefer if not shared out. As a transition to their team assignment, facilitate a brainstorm on pivoting. You can provoke learners by asking them to brainstorm features their current prototypes might have that would be in opposition to or vastly different than what they would deliver. Figure 8-13 shows a two-phase approach to developing innovative ideas using a mind map that encourages the development of bad ideas that are then organized on a 2 by 2 grid. This visual model is inspired by the idea that when we intentionally develop bad ideas, new and innovative ideas might emerge from them.

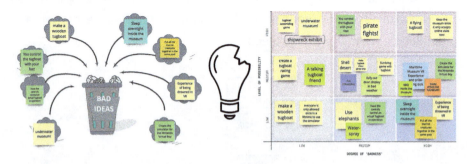

Figure 8-13. *Two-phase bad ideas brainstorms using a mind and a 2 by 2 grid contrasting level of possibility of creating the idea vs. degree of badness*

Week 8 is an opportunity for teams to present their revised project plans and for you to comment and facilitate learner feedback. In this class, it's important to allow learners to break out into teams and review their Agile Feature Board, and you can provide them with feedback particularly in relation to features they are including so that they can aim for success as they refine ideas of what the final prototype will look and feel like.

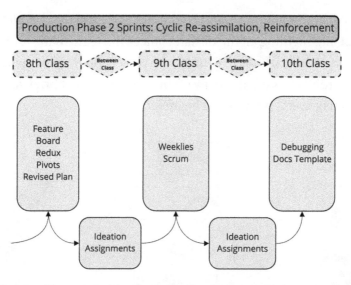

Figure 8-14. *Classes 8–10 where students enter their second major production phase*

Weeks 9 and 10 are production weeks giving learners ample time and space in class to discuss obstacles they identify in their weekly progress and for them to structure Weeklies. Weeklies are similar the idea of Dailies in various industries and have similar characteristics. Weeklies allow teams to present an aspect of their project that they would like feedback on. They function as internal user-testing only less formal. You can draw attention to user-testing protocols during this time and have them plan more formal user-tests if you think it is within scope of the project course.

Week 11 is a class focused on ensuring that learners are prepared for their final presentations and that they have begun documenting their work. Here, you can delineate all the component parts of the documentation you want them to submit. Structuring the documentation is a lesson in itself. Providing learners clear guidelines will support them immensely. Each part of the final document needs explanation as to why it should be included. What are the benefits of a final design document?

Technical documentation should be present as part of the overall design document, highlighting all the design choices the team made and why. Screenshots of assets, links to GitHub, the project plan, team makeup, the identified problem to solve, a copy of the original project brief, and the project management plan can all be included.

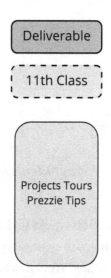

Figure 8-15. *The important second last class*

Depending on your own skill set, you can provide them with formal presentation structures that they can use to build their slide deck and practice for the last class. Their assignment is to be able to highlight their Minimum Viable Prototypes, or proof of concepts (depending on scope) for the entire class and client partner.

Week 12 is the final class and can be a celebratory one in which presentations are given to the class and client partners and short feedback cycles are facilitated.

Figure 8-16. *Final class*

In addition, you can conduct a course Retrospective to give learners an opportunity to begin reflecting on their experience in the course. This is to help them re-understand what they learned and what they will take away and hopefully apply wherever their future careers take them. An in-class Retro is also a prep for an eventual course evaluation that the college or university will encourage you to link student anonymously to in the last few weeks of the course.

In-Between Classes

In between classes, there are multiple mentoring opportunities. You can have quick check-ins with team members during the week to understand learner progress and answer questions. You can also set office hours either in-person or remotely. You can also have formal lab times where you and/or your teaching assistant can be present to support learners and guide them according to what their needs are.

Identifying the Gaps in Your Own Knowledge

You've already identified what you could teach and what gaps you might encounter when learners need to co-construct an emerging technology project together. Going through an entire teaching pipeline as has been modelled in this chapter is a good way for you to identify what you know you can teach, what you cannot teach, what you think with a little more lead time you could teach, and what you may need to have a special guest teach.

To Do: Rapidly Plot What, How, and When You Will Teach

Use the table structure in Table 8-1 to start to define what and how you will teach and plot activities over time. In terms of When you will teach an activity, consider the entire PjBL pipeline. You can also identify when you will need to secure a guest, or hire a teaching assistant for your class who could provide workshops to you and the learners.

Table 8-1. *A tool that can support the design of teaching interventions throughout a PjBL pipeline*

What needs to be taught	How you will teach it	When you will teach it
•		
•		
•		

The example of teaching learners how to code comes to mind. You may understand what a coder does, the development environment, and when they are more active and even understand when their workload is heavier and what they need to consider when it comes to scoping a project. Yet, coding may not be part of the skill set that you have. You can also survey the class in the first few weeks as to which skills they might have that could benefit everyone in the class, not just their immediate team. Should learners with specific skills need support and a budget is available, skill-specific mentors can also be sourced, along with an abundance of online resources and recommendations from colleagues of simpler coding languages less experience coders in the course may want to explore. Your greatest resource is your own community of practice, so it is important to ask for support where you feel you have the greatest gaps.

Precourse and Preproject Preparation

Precourse prep is also the main responsibility of the instructor/mentor, usually establishing contact and rapport with upcoming clients, identifying which students are well matched for which project and weighing that against what project they've identified as being of interest, correcting mistakes made in assigning the wrong student to a project, etc.

Figure 8-17. *Precourse preparation*

Client Contact As Part of Prep Work

Initial contact with a potential client (if you have one) and a general understanding of the type of digital media project you want your students to take on is a first step. If you do take on a client, you can also communicate the importance of allowing flexibility with what the learners propose and ensuring that the project is not critical path for the client partner. In other words, they are not depending on the results of the student team's efforts for their own company's projects or their funded research projects. There are many pros and some cons for taking on a real-world client partner so this should be carefully reviewed.

The clients prepare a simple one-page Brief (see Appendix 1) that outlines an initial project ask, provides a background of the company, and positions the type of project and technology as part of a problem that needs solving. This type of document serves as a one-pager that is given to learners on day one of their project semester. Where this can be improved is in how the idea is articulated and the format of the proposition. While some ambiguity will always be present, it's helpful for you to at least consider if there is enough room for learners to propose a unique solution.

Choosing Project Types

The second step is to assess the project type, client partner commitment, and capacity of student skill sets. As the project is understood more deeply, identify if the proposed project is aligned with the course learning outcomes. Depending on the personality of the client, the scope, and their propensity to be adaptable to changing their idea, the goal may also include the need to prescope the client, set expectations, get time commitments, and be clear that learners are not work for hire but are present as individuals who may be learning design for the first time. In addition, simple projects like "build me a website" will not be challenging enough for learners as there are enough web services that already offer services that can do that. If a project idea is too ambiguous, not refined enough, or simply confusing, then a decision is usually made not to do that project. Finally, you will need to manage client expectations and ensure they understand that they need flexibility, patience, and openness collaborating with students. They would benefit from also knowing that they will act as partners in the learning itself, and in some cases, as mentors.

Assigning Students to Projects

Assigning students to projects is one of the most challenging aspects of the process as you need to assign them to a project based on the following:

- The type of project some students have communicated they'd like to be on.

- Known personality clashes. This may not be identified early in the semester, but it is an important component to monitor throughout the course. You may be able to shift learners from one team to another or find other solutions for a particular student who does not function well collaboratively to contribute.

- The skill sets of the students, and their level of skill to be able to handle the anticipated challenges. This is unknown at first and requires you to investigate from the first class onward. A preclass activity could be designed that captures student skills and levels of proficiency so that by the time the first class begins you begin to get a sense of the class.

- The desire of some students to have a portfolio piece will influence the amount of work they are willing to put into their projects. This may not always be aligned among team members, and it is important to remind all learners that the priority of their PjBL experience is to learn about emerging technology development through an iterative design process that can be documented. Emphasizing the importance of documenting their process can also be affirmed as a learning outcome and tangible artifact that is assessed.

Chapter Summary

Previous chapters have proposed that you identify your mentoring strategies, what to teach, and what to mentor along a PjBL pipeline. That work and the understanding of core features of PjBL will support the development of learner competencies. These competencies will inform the criteria that will help you assess learners properly in a PjBL environment.

This chapter

- Offered a flexible template for a typical undergraduate 12–13-week PjBL course highlighting specific milestones and drawing attention to what you may need to teach within each milestone

- Included the breakdown of an entire project course pipeline to support you in starting to think about what to teach and when

- Recommended that you identify knowledge gaps that you have and think about how you might fill those gaps with either learning targeted skills, pointing to resources, or bringing in colleagues to support you when needed

Tools and Suggested Processes

- Understand and design primary milestones of a PjBL pipeline.

- Design a week-by-week breakdown of a PjBL course.

- Facilitate the identification of core values for your class and to model that process for your learner's teams.

- Leverage the Dream Home activity to provide a condensed experience of an Agile project pipeline that can also provide experience for a Wizard of Oz prototype.

- Leverage out of the box ideas and the visual model of Bad Ideas to facilitate learners to pivot intentionally, to provoke innovation.

- Conduct a gap analysis to better understand what you need to learn, what resources you need to prepare, and what support you may need to enlist from your community of practice.

Deeper Dive

Dix, A., Ormerod, T., Twidale, M., Sas, C., Silva, P. A., & McKnight, L. (2006). Why bad ideas are a good idea.

https://medium.com/tajawal/5-great-activities-to-get-your-team-excited-about-agile-b0c88f4a901a

CHAPTER 9

Know How to Assess Learners

Chapter Goal: This chapter provides a process for you to identify competencies that lead to the criteria for how a learner is more accurately assessed.

To be able to assess learners on their work in a PjBL course

You need to develop rigorous assessment criteria

So you can reach a final grade more accurately.

Previous chapters of this book have provided you with tools to break down the production pipeline into phases and identify what needs to be taught and mentored and why. When students enrolled in PjBL courses apply what they learn to the co-construction of a digital media prototype, they enact competencies. They actively engage in iterative attempts to apply what they know (and learn what they need) to a design problem they solve with others in the form of multiple versions of prototypes.

The feedback they receive from the application of skills and competencies eventually needs to be translated into some type of letter grade or percentage out of 100. This form of assessment might closely resemble performance indicators or metrics in your profession. The process used to define metrics or criteria is similar in post-secondary environments with the guiding principle that all criteria must apply to all learners.

© Patrick Parra Pennefather 2022
P. Parra Pennefather, *Mentoring Digital Media Projects*,
https://doi.org/10.1007/978-1-4842-8798-9_9

There is a process to go through to help identify the criteria that will inform an individual's grade. Those criteria are informed by what you want them to get out of the course: a combination of the skills and the competencies you anticipate learners will walk away with. Some learners will exceed your expectations, and some will underwhelm, and the median in-between will likely satisfy most of the criteria in the course as learners new to emerging technology production pipelines begin to unravel their understanding of it. You may also want to better understand the grading procedures of the department you will be working with. Asking to look at a colleague's grading rubric will help inform the design of your rubric.

What learners walk away with at the end of a PjBL pipeline are competencies usually expressed as their learning outcomes. How you assess those are the criteria that measure how well learners achieve those intended outcomes. These outcomes directly relate to how well learners applied the skills and competencies you taught and mentored in the course.

Admittedly we are being idealists when we project these intended outcomes. In collaborative PjBL courses, it's difficult to accurately measure the degree of a how well a student met all the criteria defined by all the learning outcomes. Yet, we must. An essential part of teaching a PjBL course is to design the assessment criteria that will accurately measure how well each learner demonstrated their understanding of the production pipeline. Once you've told learners what the combination of criteria and their value out of 100 will be, referred to as a rubric, you will have to stick with it until you design another course.

Process of Developing Criteria

In terms of the process of assessing how well people learn in your PjBL course, there are many approaches. Figure 9-1 depicts one process that leads to the development of assessment criteria for learners to better understand their comprehension of the many competencies and interrelated learning outcomes they acquire on a PjBL course focused on emerging technology.

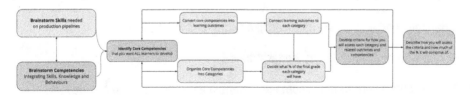

Figure 9-1. *A process of developing assessment criteria in PjBL*

Step 1: Skills Brainstorm

Create a table like in Table 9-1. Use the prompt "On a production pipeline students need to learn how to _____". Fill in the blanks. Brainstorm all the skills or specific abilities you want learners to have by the end of the 12-week course. For this, you may want to work from what you know, which means uncovering skills for each type of position you are familiar with in an emerging technology pipeline. That will likely include project management skills like Excel; Trello; coding skills in C# or C++; 3D art skills like animating, rendering, and rigging; user experience design skills like being able to plan a user-test; user interface design; and those necessary but hard-to-define in-between roles like technical artist, pipeline producer, etc. These can also be broader to all types of roles.

Note   You'll notice that one course cannot possibly teach students to learn all these abilities.

Prompt: On a production pipeline, students need to learn how to...

Table 9-1. *A list of some of the skills or abilities that learners can develop in a PjBL course*

Skill (the ability to)

Understand and apply Agile methods like scrum and Retrospectives.

Pick up what they need to get the task done.

Coder: Create a wireframe, become proficient in a coding environment, debug.

Artist: Generate mood boards, concept art, 2D or 3D assets, rig, animate.

Create low- and high-resolution prototypes.

Apply a root cause visual model to identifying a problem to be solved.

Practice storyboarding techniques.

Develop psychographic profiles.

Step 2: Relating Skills to Competencies

Add a new column on the same table. Identify some of the competencies that relate to the skills that learners would need to develop to contribute to an emerging technology team. Competencies are more general referring to the capacities that all members of a team could potentially acquire. There can be competencies like problem-solving, creative thinking, collaborating, and communicating, managing, etc. Some competencies encompass skills students need to acquire. It is important to delineate the difference so you can properly create rubrics that assess competencies vs. skills.

Prompt: On a production pipeline, students need to learn how to...

Table 9-2. *Associate skills with competencies, the capacities learners can develop during a PjBL course*

Skill (the ability to)	Competency (the applied capacity to...)
Understand and apply Agile methods such as the format of User Stories, scrum, Sprint goals and planning, task estimation, and Retrospectives.	Manage the time they put into the execution of tasks and features that contribute to different types of prototypes that fulfill a user's need.
Learn specific skills to achieve what they need to get the task done.	Self-regulate their learning throughout the PjBL pipeline.
Coder: Create a wireframe, become proficient in a coding environment, debug.	Design, innovate, iterate, and problem-solve to program interactions within an identified coding environment that affords the interactions needed to solve a user need or problem.
Artist: Generate mood boards, concept art, 2D or 3D assets, rig, animate.	Design, make creative offers, be creative, and iterate in order to visualize an application and provide visual feedback to a user that fulfills an identified need.
Create low- and high-resolution prototypes.	Co-construct different representations of a project at varied levels of fidelity corresponding to identified user needs that answer design questions, whose value is affirmed or validated through user-testing.

Step 3: Distill Core Competencies

From the first two brainstorms, you now need to plot those competencies that would be beneficial for every type of role on a production pipeline. There is a need to generalize or find common ground because when you develop learning outcomes and relate these to assessment criteria that form your rubric, every learner needs to be assessed using the same criteria. While their role on a team might be a programmer, you wouldn't necessarily assess them solely for their ability to code, but rather, their capacity to contribute to their team's final project through their defined role and how well they aligned with team production processes like prototyping, and management processes like Agile. The difference between skills and competencies is key in properly defining assessment criteria in PjBL environments.

From the table, you can now begin to condense the competencies learners will develop throughout the entire course. Remember, they are not as specific as the skills, although competencies are achieved through the application of targeted skills in the context of co-constructing prototypes that solve a human-centered problem. Figure 9-2 is one such competency map that I've developed over the years that you can draw from to customize your own.

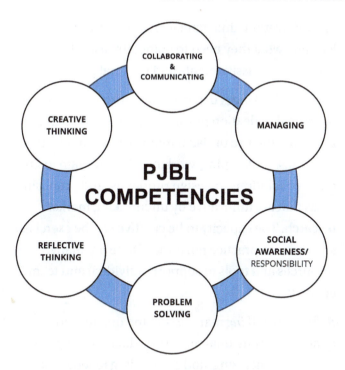

Figure 9-2. *Six core competencies drawn from over 45 projects during the past 15 years of PjBL courses*

All team members no matter their role, the tasks they perform, or the skills they need to learn to complete those tasks enact these six interrelated core competencies during a PjBL technology development pipeline:

- *Collaborating* with others by sharing and receiving ideas; finding alignment or complementarity with ideas, vision, direction, scope, and process; and engaging in persistent *Communication* that demands they respond in a timely fashion to one another.

- *Managing* their project and associated responsibilities using Agile, managing team relationships by applying Scrum and remote communication channels, and managing their own learning process including self-motivation, time management, self-care, and learning what they need to complete tasks that contribute to assignments and the final project.

- *Creative thinking* is demonstrated through persistent offers in the ideation phase of a project, through the adoption and use of visual models and proposing new ones, prototyping, working with the team to find creative solutions to design problems, and proposing ideas that are innovative by undertaking market research. The capacity to be creative can be exercised and through practice nurtured. There are many resources and tools to support individual and team creativity.

- *Reflective thinking* manifests in the quality and quantity of individual reflection, documenting that reflection, analyzing, and responding to feedback about their work, and their performance. In addition, contributions to team Retrospectives demonstrate a capacity to remain engaged with the project at every phase of co-construction.

- *Social awareness and responsibility* are demonstrated by everyone's desire to build and maintain a team culture, ensuring that protocols of communication and idea sharing and reception are defined, that team core values are respected, and that care is taken to support one another throughout the co-construction process. What learners decide to build is just as important. Teaching them the broader impact and uses of the projects they create is useful to facilitate discussion about.

- *Problem-solving* combines many important features
  of PjBL including the development of team heuristics
  (or methods to solve problems that come up), the use
  of iterative design processes to test out prototypes
  and gauge their potential to solve a problem that
  is identified, and a process to solve team or client
  problems that might surface.

Step 4: Develop Associated Subcompetencies

Figure 9-3 represents a more detailed version of the competency map with some common subcompetencies. These subcompetencies can be taught and mentored through the various individual and group assignments learners undertake and are enacted throughout the project development pipeline. Some subcompetencies intersect across the core competencies depicted in the visual model.

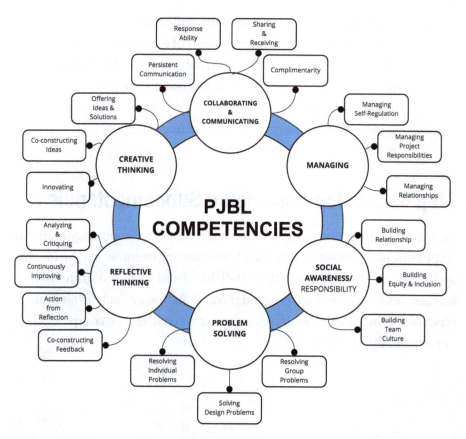

Figure 9-3. *Competencies and subcompetencies enacted during a PjBL pipeline*

Collaborating and Communicating

- *Response ability* is the capacity for learners to be present and available to respond to offers and communicate needs, in-person and through remote social channels. The timing of their responses to each other, individual and team responsibility for designing effective communication channels, the quality and quantity of client partner communication and responsiveness, and a team's persistent communication with you can all form part of the criteria of assessment.

- *Sharing and receiving* ideas persistently over the course of the entire semester can be observed and, in some cases, have been quantified by PjBL instructors. While you don't necessarily have to go to this extreme, you will need to take notes as to the quantity and, importantly, the quality of offers learners make. In terms of receiving offers from other learners, you can assess their capacity to listen, how they respond to suggestions from their peers, whether they understand the offer or critique, whether they build on someone else's ideas, and how intentionally they design and activate their own communication patterns.

- *Persistent communication* is an essential part of a PjBL course, and it is crucial that learners practice communicating in-between classes. That can be achieved through various mediums including email, social work channels, etc. A clear indicator of team's communication is how clear a project's goals are when a team of learners presents a status update in classes.

- *Complementarity* is the action that learners take to compromise impulses for the purposes of finding alignment and cohesion with their team. This is a negotiated process and may take an entire semester for a team to develop. Assessment can be based on the quality of team alignment, how learners achieved that alignment, and individual interest in persistently seeking alignment, in addition to how well the team aligns with the vision of the client partner, as demonstrated through making propositions as to how they will solve the problem at hand.

- *Managing self-regulation* is the practiced capacity for learners to manage their own learning. This competency is well researched in the field of education and a feature of PjBL is that it has been linked for many years to self-regulation. Signs of a self-regulatory learner include lessening their dependency on the instructor over time, learning what they need to complete tasks and solve problems, becoming aware of their own learning process, finding buy-in with a project as a key indicator of self-motivation, and taking initiative to participate in class activities without the need to be asked each time.

- *Managing project* responsibilities including tasks and throughout the entire production pipeline is difficult for individuals let alone teams to master in one 12-week course. The degree of responsibility for all the tasks they each must take on and relate to the features they co-construct with others is one assessment indicator. Are they contributing to the scrum board? Are they communicating changes in the status of their tasks? Are they following scrum? To what degree did they properly plan out the project scope overall, and the smaller sprints over time?

- *Managing their relationships* throughout a project course is another competency that learners will enact as they negotiate vision and responsibility and develop team culture.

Creative Thinking

- *Offering ideas and solutions* during all phases of a pipeline can form different criteria that contribute to final assessment of their project. This can include the Ideation or Discovery phase where initial brainstorms offer tangible artifacts that you can observe. During the production pipeline, creative solutions to problems, feedback to improve a learner's project, and other projects can all form part of the criteria through which you measure this competency.

- *Co-constructing ideas* is related to creative offers in addition to the capacity for learners to share and receive offers. Understanding that their combined contributions form part of their assessment is helpful.

- *Innovating* in the context of PjBL is demonstrated through a learner's capacity to rapidly research what solutions have been applied on similar projects and then make propositions that are not conventional or have not been achieved before.

Reflective Thinking

- *Analyzing and critiquing* the work of others in addition to their own work can be captured during Retrospectives and observed within each class.

- *Continuously improving* work and behavioral habits throughout a PjBL process is another criterion you can assign assessment to.

- *Action from reflection* is a key capacity that supports a rapid prototyping process. The action that results from reflection can include an immediate change and improvement of team process, team dynamics, individual performance, quality of work, etc.

- *Co-constructing feedback* with others in captured Retrospectives supports learners in reviewing what they said about the project and the quantity of offers they made. The key outcome of teams that provide one another constructive feedback is an accelerated learning and self-awareness.

Social Awareness and Responsibility

- *Building relationships* with each other and the client partner who represents a community of practice is an important capacity to strengthen. Interest in each other's work, supporting team members, and being respectful at all phases of a PjBL course are the indicators that can lead to criteria that you develop.

- *Building equity and inclusion* is in part an inherent component in the design of a PjBL course. The development of a flat culture where leadership can be rotated, a decision-making framework, where all learners have a voice that is heard and affirmed, demonstrated respect and awareness of bias, microaggressions, and how learners speak to one another are all capacities that can be facilitated through Core Values, Rules of Play activities, and persistent check-ins with teams. Bringing awareness to microaggressions that can surface because of the

pressure students face working with the unknown and
with people they have just met is beneficial. Supporting
learners to acknowledge and communicate aesthetic
and bias with one another can also support you as you
match students together. The capacity for learners to
abide by those behaviors they tolerate and those they
do not demonstrates the assimilation of this important
competency. Finally, no matter how you identify or
represent yourself in the world, it is useful to bring in
contrasting voices so that learners have exposure to
different opinions and perspectives.

- *Building team culture* is similar to building
  relationships in addition to equity and inclusion.
  Developing a sense of culture requires a commitment
  to creating bonds with team members, and that
  bond can be long lasting. Attention should be paid to
  supporting students in the development of their team
  culture and showing use cases in industry where this is
  the case is helpful in reinforcing its importance.

Problem-Solving

- *Solving design problems* is a key subcompetency in
  PjBL courses and students will quickly learn that their
  individual process of solving problems (heuristics)
  will be different than that of others. Important is
  to persistently draw the learner's attention on how
  they solve problems and how they negotiate solving
  problems with others. That awareness will support
  them in exploring new ways of doing so. More than
  likely, expect learners to have difficulty identifying

a problem to solve. Sometimes they may go for an obvious or surface problem and you may need to guide them through some type of root cause visual model to support them in going a bit deeper.

- *Resolving group problems* may or may not emerge for you and the teams of students you facilitate. Often, if given a sufficient number of tools and strategies to find alignment and resolve disagreements in the design process, learners will resolve challenges on their own. Where and when they do manifest is common enough. Problems tend to show up when learners start out working with each other especially if they've not worked collaboratively before. Some students are unable to deliver on what they say they will do. This will inevitably create friction with other team members. Problems also tend to surface when communication patterns with team members are erratic so ensure that your assessment criteria in your overall project grade clearly define team communication.

- *Resolving individual problems* can be more challenging but at times they do come up. These tend to be related to an individual's capacity to balance all their courses and also their ability to maintain their mental health throughout the process. Recurring core office hours every week will be helpful to offer learners who need the time an opportunity to meet with you and discuss how they are doing with the course, etc.

Identifying Learning Outcomes from Demonstrated Competencies

To articulate learning outcomes specific to each phase of production, it's a good idea to chart the competencies you've articulated along the major parts of the PjBL course pipeline. Some will repeat and others may not. This is another way to test the validity of the competencies you've developed against the activities and interactions you're in the process of designing that enact those competencies.

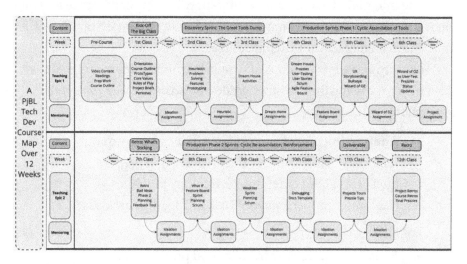

Figure 9-4. *A 12–13 week undergraduate PjBL course*

Learning outcomes should explain to the learner what they will learn in the course overall and that they will be able to do so because of taking your course. You may want to create twelve to begin with, each of them corresponding to distinct or mixed core and subcompetencies you identify each week. Some may repeat over two or more weeks. To make each statement succinct, it is common to begin each sentence with an active present tense verb that can observe and measure, followed by the content learners would perform the task for. Following the subject content is a description of how well a student needs to be in a task. Next is a condition of performance such as "with limited supervision."

Precourse Learning Outcomes

You can even create learning outcomes from competencies you think students will enact before they have the first class with you. The precourse content you create will also reflect knowledge you want learners to undertake before they can take on a project together. There's a lot of knowledge you may need to provide about process, big picture, expectations, etc. This is where asynchronous media like the outline of your course, video and articles, blog posts, and other types of knowledge will come into play. That precourse content will help set the stage for what you want to accomplish and may even accelerate the understanding of what is expected of learners in the course.

Work through a few versions of what a learning outcome might look like in this case using the four-part guide of *measurable action*, *content*, *description*, and *condition*.

- **Analyze** (*measurable action*) available asynchronous materials before the first class (*content*) to prepare questions about emerging technology pipelines (*task description*) that you'll ask during the first class (*condition or the why*).

- **Recall** key takeaways from several preclass videos to pass a short quiz that will be given during the first class.

- **Contribute** what you've learned from the first reading based on a prompt in an online discussion thread.

Discovery Sprint Learning Outcomes

Once they start the first couple of weeks of classes and you teach them what's necessary to successfully move toward your intended learning outcomes, there will be several emerging competencies that will be helpful to predict. Identify those competencies that come from engaging in the

Ideation or Discovery phase. These may relate to the subcompetencies of communicating and collaborating and social awareness/responsibility that were proposed in the PjBL competency model proposed earlier.

Table 9-3. *Articulating competencies and subcompetencies as a learning outcome*

Competence	Learning Outcome
Listening to your team members' ideas and building on them	Build on other people's ideas when you brainstorm and present the results in the class for peer feedback.
Communicating persistently with team members in-between classes	Demonstrate how you and your team members communicate effectively in-between classes and share communication process to the entire class.
Finding alignment and complementarity with your team members' ideas	Prioritize ideas in negotiation with others to propose aligned projects to the class for critical feedback.
Building an equitable and inclusive team culture	Identify and categorize Core Team Values and explain how you and your team will integrate them throughout your project.

Production Phase(s) Learning Outcomes

You'll likely notice similar competencies being demonstrated in the Production phases of your PjBL course as learners move through a cyclic process of creating, presenting, and reflecting. What are some learning outcomes you can compose based on Agile, iterative design, and prototyping? Which competencies would they correspond to? You can apply the same tables to all phases of a production pipeline.

Table 9-4. *Develop your own competencies and work on articulating them as learning outcomes*

Competence	Learning Outcome
•	
•	
•	

Broader Learning Outcomes

As a final step, you can generate broad learning outcome statements from grouping the previously articulated learning outcomes that you've identified during each phase of production. These can then inform the criteria that will form part of your evaluation rubric. Here are some examples directly related to PjBL environments to start you off:

- Deliver a project at a negotiated level of capability and completion within time and resource constraints, with limited supervision.

- Solve assigned design problems with others by creating prototypes whose subsequent versions improve after they are presented for feedback.

- Apply human-centered design visual models through weekly assignments and present them in class for peer evaluation.

- Implement an Agile process every week and show tangible artifacts related to your project plan and individually completed tasks for review.

- Compare and contrast knowledge gained through targeted readings, articulate your understanding of them, and respond to others in writing.

Agile Retrospectives As a Key Formative Assessment Tool

Grading within post-secondary PjBL courses, while painful, is necessary. Learners require a percentage out of 100 for assignments and how they collaborated with one another on a project. Combined assessments lead to their final assessment. While we may have gotten used to a different type of assessment model in the workplace (e.g., performance metrics that inform salary raises, retention, promotion, or firing), in academic institutions the goal of assessment is to give students an idea of how they are doing with the knowledge and knowing in the course they are experiencing. Higher grades affirm that learners are developing and understanding their course content and how to apply it, and lower grades communicate to learners that something is missing in their understanding.

So how do we even get close to comparing workplace assessment with assessment that occurs in learning environments?

We can get a good idea of a particular, performance and behavior pattern over time and convert that effort into a grade. This is usually a biased interpretation, so we need to balance that reading of a person's performance, with methods to grade learners using rubrics. Rubrics are composed of criteria that inform how a learner should be graded based on their capacity to fulfill those criteria. Composing criteria that relate to the competencies and learning outcomes of the course then are an essential part of post-secondary PjBL grading procedures. A common approach is to assess learners formatively, that is, along the way instead of solely giving them a final summative evaluation at the end of a semester. Keep in mind that learners will require a final grade but how you get to that assessment is similar to the idea of milestones that are used in many different types of Agile production environments.

The idea of Sprints in Agile provides, a cyclic way to assess learners and provide that feedback to them so they have the opportunity to improve. Plan a minimum of three milestones, although two are more common. The additional assessment milestone can occur directly after Discovery in week 3, to give feedback to individual learners on their performance, to understand and communicate where they might need support, and to give them feedback on how they can improve their performance, and thus, their grade. The second assessment milestone should occur just after the middle of the semester and likely in week 7 after learners have presented some type of prototype they have worked on together. The second milestone is vital in providing individuals and teams an idea as to where they are at, so they can reflect on effort vs. results, and give them an opportunity to also provide you feedback as to what obstacles they have toward doing better.

This approach sends the message, that grading goes both ways and can help you to help learners to remove obstacles they may have that are based on the design of instruction that evolves over the semester. It's essential at this stage to really listen to what is happening with teams of individuals so that you may support them in improving. If you discover that most of your learners are missing some essential knowledge, or something "didn't stick," it may not solely be their fault. A general rule of play is if you find that most of the teams that you mentor missed the point of an activity, or have not embodied Agile (for example), then that is likely a reflection on the methods of delivery, and you may need to adjust your future classes accordingly.

You are also assessing how rapidly learners are picking things up. To do so, you can also put interventions in place to test the class. This can be as simple and effective as a quiz at the beginning of subsequent classes where learners are tested for their knowledge on material covered the week before. Even more effectively, you may also choose to conduct spot tests without any premeditated warning to test their knowledge in the present. Quizzes given at the beginning of a class are also strategic method, to ensure attendance.

Testing Bias

No system of grading is perfect. Sometimes nuances are missed in a student's performance or an assignment that can make the difference between a learner's expectation of their grade and the reality of your perception of them and the grade that accompanies their effort and understanding of an assigned activity. Work from what you know and associate each grading level with an accompanying reflection as to what it might mean in your own workplace.

- **An A-range grade** will reward exceptional performance that might even make the candidate hirable should they want a job in the industry you are a part of. Integration with course content is high and their participation in your class has been persistently active. You'd have no hesitation writing up a recommendation letter.

- **A B-range grade** shows good performance, but something is still missing from that performance for you to give them a higher assessment. There is a grasp of some of the tools but not all. Behavior might be unpredictable, including problems with punctuality, degrees of low participation with the course content. You might consider a recommendation letter but only if they are willing to step up. These are the types of personas at jobs that if cuts had to be made, they may or may not make that cut depending on how their performance compares to the rest.

- **A C-range grade** is the result of barely passable performance and learners with this grade are not memorable. They have barely contributed, nor completed assignments on time. They have likely missed more than one class and not explained why. They have rarely participated in the class when present, and it is unclear what they contributed to their project team. You would not recommend this student to any of your peers in the industry until they can demonstrate change.

- Anything below a C gets worse from here.

So how do you arrive at those assessments?

Well one method, which simultaneously tests your bias, especially if more familiar with assessment in the workplace that is driven by different types of variables, is to fulfill two complementary types of grading processes. The first tasks you with giving a *gut* grade. What does your gut instinct tell you about a learner's performance in the course? That gut instinct is usually based on your own professional experience and/or other PjBL courses that you've taught. There is a comparative scale happening. We've all had the experience of having to assess an amazing performer and at times they raise the bar for others to reach. Of course, the reality of assessment in an undergraduate PjBL will be different than that of a Master program. That's why we need to temper our gut instinct with the rubrics we've designed. They help guide our assessment to ensure a fair evaluation is provided to a learner that is based on assignments, their collaboration, communication, and management competencies that inform the caliber of contribution to a final project, and their participation in each class and in-between classes.

This second approach involves quite a bit of preparation and is critical to implement as it provides a robust framework with metrics that can show learners how you came to grade them and reduce personal bias.

Those biases may come from workplace environments where a certain level of performance is expected. Students may need to learn what that means when it comes to a 3-credit 10–15 hour a week commitment. Some may show signs of the kind of performance you are used to but anticipate that there will be less students in this category and more who need support in improving performance over time. A low assessment is not a good motivator. You will also have to measure your own expectations within a learning environment that will likely be unfamiliar territory. To counter potential biases, determine what assignments will contribute to a final grade, break down those assignments, scale in-class and remote contributions that contribute to a participation grade, and create a rubric for the project itself as well as the methods you asked them to follow when you delineated the tools, approach, and process at the beginning of the semester. Dividing up the different criteria that combine to make up an individual's final assessment is your rubric.

Rubrics

Rubrics are formed by the combined criteria that associate a percentage out of 100 of a learner's participation, collaboration, and capacity to deliver assignments in a PjBL course. Rubrics are also formed from the criteria that combine to assess the assignments that learners are assigned. Criteria relate to the core competencies you define and the associated learning outcomes that you've designed.

Participation Rubrics

Looking at participation rubrics, first locate the various interactions that learners have had throughout the PjBL pipeline that a grade can be associated with. These can include the following:

- Asynchronous interactions contributing to discussion threads based on supplementary reading materials. These can include the offers a learner makes and the quantity and quality of their responses to others.

- Communicating and collaborating with each other during project time that may be made known to you through participation in social work channels, observation in labs, and one-on-one midterm peer and self-evaluations.

- In-class participation that can define individual offers made during the class that contributed to discussion of a subject, reflection, and planned partner or group activities.

Once you uncover what interactions you design in the course that can be assessed, you need to create a single scale with all criteria to be included in the evaluation being considered.

Note   Observations you make are most accurate when they are coupled with documented notes of what you observe. Relying on your memory for something you observed three weeks or even one week prior may not accurately represent what occurred.

In the examples just used, you might create the criteria in Table 9-5.

***Table* 9-5.** *Competencies on the left inform the criteria you decide on to evaluate those competencies*

Competency embedded within learning outcomes	Criteria that contribute to its assessment
Asynchronous interactions contributing to discussion threads based on supplementary reading materials. These can include the offers a learner makes and the quantity and quality of their responses to others.	• Word count although pay attention to repetition and potential English as an additional language articulation. • Quality of offering, which can correspond to the prompt you gave students. • Responses to others. Beyond likes, a better way to assess learner responses to one another is by the quality and depth of that response and how they addressed the initial post they respond to. • Comprehension is better thought of as a student's capacity to articulate their thoughts clearly. Once again, you may need to reevaluate an offer made by an English as an additional language learner and support them where necessary.

(continued)

Table 9-5. (*continued*)

Competency embedded within learning outcomes	Criteria that contribute to its assessment
Communicating and collaborating with each other during project time that may be made known to you through participation in social work channels, observation in labs, and one-on-one midterm peer and self-evaluations.	• Individual assignments with subcriteria well defined and scaled in comparison to the others. • Team assignments if it is clear what learner completed what part of the assignment. • Participation in social channels including offers and responses students make to one another with regard to project tasks, insights, solutions, and removing obstacles. • Evidence of task completion, which can be assessed when learners present and communicate what they did to complete a task. • Observation in team breakouts as to who is contributing and in what ways they are contributing to conversation or brainstorming. Ensure that observations are documented. • Peer evaluation weighed by quality and depth. • Self-evaluation weighed against peer and instructor evaluation for accuracy.
In-class participation that can define individual offers made during the class that contributed to discussion of a subject, reflection, and planned partner or group activities.	• In-class contribution to any discussion including reflections that follow in-class activities. • Group discussion based on observation and capture. • In-class activities including rapid prototyping, and the use of visual models. • In-class presentations and individual contributions to those presentations. • Q&A sessions that follow in-class presentation of assignments or weeklies.

In the examples provided in Table 9-5, the specific criteria are then weighed and inform a grade out of a number you decide. Each assignment forms part of the final course rubric. Each of these criteria informs the final grade for that assignment. Each assignment contributes to your final course rubric. Using the first entry in the table, you might assign 10% of the entire course assessment based on learner responses to readings that you assigned.

Assignment Rubrics

When we define criteria for assignments in PjBL, there will be several types of assignments to consider:

- Individual assignments that are specific to each class and usually submitted prior to the next class. Types include visual models, different types of reflection, etc.

- Group assignments that can include visual models, prototypes of different kinds, processes related to the final project, the final project, and documentation of the final project and its process.

Bear in mind that a challenging part of PjBL courses is to individuate grading as much as possible. Since projects are group efforts, group assignments and grades will likely all be the same grade for every student. An exception are self and peer evaluations reinforcing their inclusion in any defined rubric. Individual vs. group assessments are important to consider as you design the final weight and balance of your rubrics.

Collaboration Rubrics

In many collaborative-oriented PjBL senate-approved courses, there is usually a collaboration criterion that can be added. For these criteria, you can create subcriteria that include peer evaluation, client evaluation, self-evaluation, contribution to the final project based on submitted evidence of completed tasks and assignments, evidence of use on a social media work channel, etc. You may also want to include your assessment of an individual's accurate self-evaluation, based on how peers evaluated that individual, in addition to their observed participation and performance.

Course Rubrics

The three main criteria discussed earlier (participation, assignments, collaboration) that form part of your course evaluation for each student need to correspond to the following:

- Identified competencies and related learning outcomes

- The balance between individual and group grading with more weight given to individual assessment

- The weight between the three main criteria of participation, assignment, and collaboration

- Any subcriteria to better break down a competency into subcompetencies

The following text is one version to distribute the weight of each criteria:

Participation: 30% (attendance, punctuality, participation in-class discussion, participation in class activities, remote participation)

Collaboration: 30% (weekly collaboration with others in group meetings, contribution to group assignments, communication with team members, peer evaluation, self-evaluation, application of in-class activities to remote ones)

Assignments: 40% (completion of in-between class assignments, completion of assigned team tasks, contribution to asynchronous discussion posts, final project)

Total 100%

Assessment Milestones

Plotting multiple assessment milestones to give learners a sense of how they are doing is a strategic way to calm them down and make them feel that they are being properly assessed. The simplest timeline is to design for two formal assessment points in the semester. The first is a midterm assessment providing learners with a letter grade, and explanation as to how you came to it, and a visual explanation using your designed rubrics. The second happens at the end of the semester. You have a choice at that point to simply submit their grade a week after the course through some type of formal grading system that the university you are working with has created, or to meet with each student one-on-one so there are no surprises, or at least that the grade you have calculated is close to what they imagined. By providing a midterm assessment with clear criteria as to how to improve their grade, by the end of the semester, there should be no real surprises.

Iterating on the Course Outline

Everything you have learned in this and previous chapters is meant to provide you with the essential design ingredients that can then be condensed and communicated to learners as a course outline. Course outlines represent your contract with learners and summarize the core elements, so it is important to define some essential components:

- Details on the course time, location, and who is teaching it.

- Overview of the course.

- The fist component of a universal statement the university or college you teach at has the language for that you cut and paste.

- A course description, which forms the overview of what you will teach.

- Anticipated learning outcomes that in most cases take a specific form.

- A week-by-week course overview with activities planned.

- Some type of written statement of expectations of those who enroll including the number of weekly hours, the nature of the course, some Rules of Play around attendance, and participation in class.

- A rubric that breaks down how learners will be graded with as much detail as you think necessary.

- A second universal that describes university policies around cheating, behaviors toward others, and a number or email to launch complaints should they surface.

Each chapter has prepared you in one way or the other to be able to create a course outline as a tangible prototype that you can iterate on. The course overview is the first step. It involves a short paragraph description of what they'll learn and how they'll learn it combined with what they'll get out of it. Including broad learning outcomes is usually the next text entry. This is usually followed by some Rules of Play for your course, which may include comments on attendance, timeliness, supplies, etc. Learners will benefit from a week-by-week breakdown of activities with suggested themes and any other visuals that give them a strong sense of the entire semester. These can be placed in table with dates, class theme if there is one, and a list of activities. I've found it helpful to also list assignments particularly larger ones along with due dates so learners can plan their schedule with the many other courses they will be taking simultaneously.

This section is usually followed by a detail of the assessment criteria and in some ways pointing to attendance and what happens if students do not attend regularly. Your grading rubric with all detailed criteria is what follows. The more detail, the better as learners will have a strong sense of how they will be assessed. Following these parts of the course, what is left are a list of readings and university policies that usually address respectful behavior, mental wellness, university resources, and plagiarism.

Chapter Summary

In the process of assessing learners who learn new skills and their capacity to apply them (competencies) when solving design-oriented problems, numerous obstacles may prevent learners from understanding process, specific content, or even what they are supposed to do. Bear in mind that learners are used to more structured courses where each class is fairly delineated from the first to the last, with very little changes to the course content. Your capacity to plan for learner obstacles and remove them will support a more spontaneous learning design and impact your ongoing assessment. For example, if students have not been given activities that can teach them how to build a Wizard of Oz prototype and they submit their incomplete interpretation of the assignment, it may be difficult and even unfair to assess. Appendix 2 some obstacles that are common in PjBL environments, particularly those focused on developing emerging technologies.

This chapter

- Detailed a method to get to a rubric that can assess learners in a PjBL course

- Suggested that most learners who enroll in a PjBL course tend to be more interested in the experience, the feedback that you provide, and the collaborative features

- Highlighted that there is always an expectation to provide a final grade since the course is situated in a post-secondary institution

- Recommended that feedback be provided along the way with designed milestones

Tools and Suggested Processes

- Develop success criteria using a three-step process that helps you identify what students should learn and the know-how they develop the capacity for, demonstrated as competencies.

- Integrate and expand upon six common categories of competencies to develop learning outcomes.

- Develop assessment criteria based on how learners will demonstrate the degree to which they achieve your identified learning outcomes.

- Test your own bias by creating a rubric that can more accurately assess learner performance throughout the course.

- Plot multiple assessment milestones to give learners a sense of how they are progressing as the way of learning in PjBL will be quite unfamiliar.

- Iterate weekly on the course outline as you change what you teach to adapt to student needs and responses to what came before.

Deeper Dive

Helle, L., Tynjälä, P., & Olkinuora, E. (2006). Project-based learning in post-secondary education–theory, practice and rubber sling shots. *Higher education, 51*(2), 287-314.

Chang, C. C., & Tseng, K. H. (2011). Using a web-based portfolio assessment system to elevate project-based learning performances. *Interactive Learning Environments, 19*(3), 211-230.

Trauth-Nare, A., & Buck, G. (2011). Assessment for learning: Using formative assessment in problem-and project-based learning.

Mahasneh, A. M., & Alwan, A. F. (2018). The Effect of Project-Based Learning on Student Teacher Self-Efficacy and Achievement. *International Journal of Instruction, 11*(3), 511-524.

Lin, J. W., Tsai, C. W., Hsu, C. C., & Chang, L. C. (2021). Peer assessment with group awareness tools and effects on project-based learning. *Interactive Learning Environments, 29*(4), 583-599.

CHAPTER 10

Conclusion

The content of this book has provided you with strategies, techniques, and templates that are intended to support your design, teaching, and mentoring of a PjBL course. The processes can be applied to the development of emerging technologies or any technology for that matter. What is important is to learn from what many excellent educators have applied in the past to design a learning environment that will be beneficial to a student's educational experience, and one that will prepare them for and possibly accelerate their transition as central members of a digital media community of practice.

This book finishes with a story to consider as you bravely go forth in the many rewarding adventures you will have teaching and mentoring a PjBL course.

> *And so it happens that a person wanted to be a student but there were no teachers that they could study with who were worthy of their intelligence. They heard of a famous monk but the journey there would be long and perilous. They went anyway ignoring the advice of their closest friends. "That's stupid," they replied. "Why would I stay here and suffocate with all the ignorance around me?" Off they went and halfway up a mountain, in a teeny tiny village, the would-be-disciple ran into a grizzly old thing picking berries. "Old thing" they called out, "where can I find this monk of a thousand names?". The grizzly growled back "Help me pick the rest of these berries before dark rude one. Eat them with me and I will take you*

© Patrick Parra Pennefather 2022
P. Parra Pennefather, *Mentoring Digital Media Projects*,
https://doi.org/10.1007/978-1-4842-8798-9_10

there tomorrow morning." But the not-yet-student wouldn't have it. "Bah! Nice try. I don't have time for berries. Besides you look so thin, you'd probably eat me." and they walked on. Night came and when almost up and over the mountain, they encountered a blind woman. "Old thing," they yelled. "I've been on this road for days, almost at the top of this so-called famous mountain and still no monk of a thousand names. Tell me where I can find him." The mole replied, "Help this blind old lady back down to the village impetuous one. I'll cook you a nice meal and, in the morning, I can show you the way." But the student wasn't going to fall for that. "Ha! How can a blind woman guide me? I don't have time for this, mole." And on they went until exhausted and hungry. They travelled for days down one mountain and up another until so weak from not eating that they fell asleep in a prickly pear cactus field. As the sun barely woke the summer sky, the would-be-but-not-yet disciple was abruptly awoken by a stick poking at their leg. "Ow ow ow, why are you doing that you old wood-pecker?". The older man replied, "Because you were not yet awake and missing the sound of the bees kissing flowers and singing to the barely morning sun sleepy one. Help me collect the honey and eat with me." The student muttered: "Not a chance woodpecker. Go bother someone else with your incessant pecking. I must continue my journey." Apparently, they are still roaming the mountains and have been called the rude one, the impetuous one, the sleepy one, the hungry one, and many hundreds more.

(Old monk's tale, unknown source)

APPENDIX 1

Visual Models

The following visual models and tables are referenced in the book and some have been discussed. They represent different types of design thinking tools and have different uses depending on what phase you are in production. Preceding the visual model, an explanation as to when and why you use them will be included.

Ideation

The following visual models are useful when it comes to the development of new ideas that are focused around a project learners will take on.

Mind Mapping

You can use the general structure of a mind map which centralizes a main idea or theme in the center, then ideas related to that central idea, or theme are brainstormed. Mind maps can be used to generate ideas about a project, features, tasks, Rules of Play, etc. The first example is a mind map that was used in Chapter 1 to brainstorm known unknowns that you find in the workplace. In Chapter 2, you used the "Mentoring Is" prompt to brainstorm your own definitions of mentoring.

© Patrick Parra Pennefather 2022
P. Parra Pennefather, *Mentoring Digital Media Projects*,
https://doi.org/10.1007/978-1-4842-8798-9

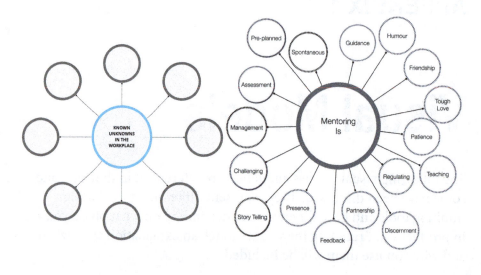

Venn Diagrams

Venn diagrams like the one used in Chapter 2 show commonalities between two opposite or sometimes polar ideas and concepts. Venn diagrams can be used to understand aligned definitions between what a client might think about a project and what a team might. They can reconcile differences in opinion, show complementarity between two types of target users, etc.

Landscape Models

Landscape visual models are also referred to as visual metaphors and attempt to position ideas graphically to guide participants and create resonance with the key characteristics that are represented. An example in this book is the What IF visual model developed by the author that allows participants to brainstorm ideas while guessing how complicated those ideas might be to manifest as a project or prototype. The following figures show the template on the left and its application in a real-world situation on the right.

Human-Centered Visual Models

There are many types of visual models that are all helpful in orienting learners to persistently think of who they are building their prototypes for. A Persona visual model is like a fancy mind map with the targeted user placed in the center and characteristics of that user coming out from them. Storyboarding is also a common tool that can be used to depict anything from a Day in the Life of a potential user to a Customer Journey map that shows how a user finds the interacts with the product you are selling.

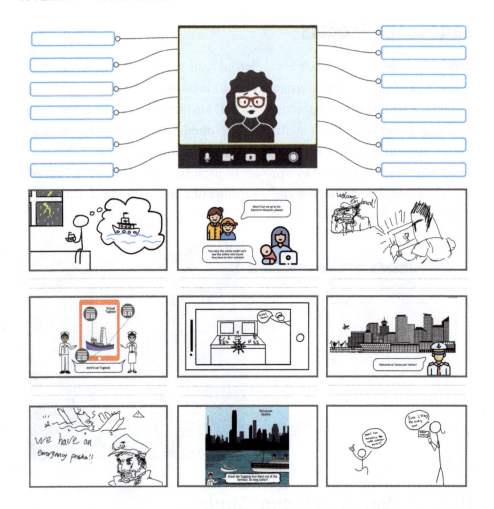

Prioritization

There are many different types of tables and grids you can use to prioritize anything from features to tasks or other ideas. The following Bullseye model can be complemented with more specific labeling of each ring as shown in the figure.

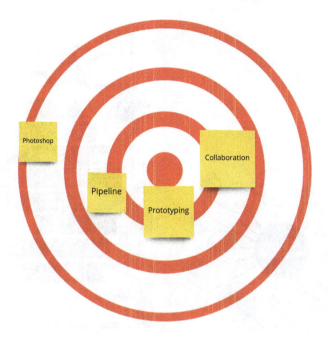

Tools to Build Team Culture

Equally important are a series of visual models that can support teams to build and sustain their culture. The first step is to generate Core Team Values that students contribute to. These allow students to then generate team Rules of Play from them. From an initial brainstorm, statements can be created that become more specific and inform a team agreement or project charter that each team member signs off on.

Production: Agile Tools

There are many types of tools, grids, tables, and Venn diagrams that can be used to support and enhance Agile teams as they enter into a production phase. Once they are clear on the project they will undertake, they can use a Scrum Board to delineate tasks needed To Do, those In-progress, and those that are done. Some teams add a fourth column for Backlog items. The Scrum Board can also be combined with the Bullseye to prioritize backlog items.

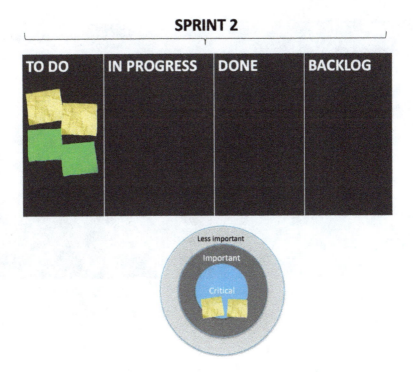

Scrum board combined with a Bullseye map allows teams to prioritize which backlog tasks and/or features they want to bring into the next Sprint.

Retrospectives

Visual models that capture Retrospectives are also very useful for teams to center their reflections around and to reference at a later time when useful. There are many types that generally try and capture what worked well during a Sprint and what could be improved upon. Patterns can develop during Retrospectives, which can help teams navigate teams to improve performance, make changes, etc. The following model is an excerpt from an end of semester Retrospective that can also be used to give you insights on the overall learner UX.

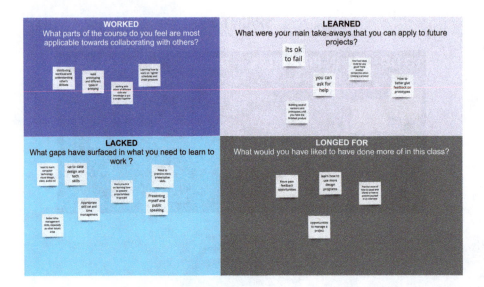

APPENDIX 2

Know How to Anticipate and Remove Obstacles

To improve the learner experience in the PjBL course that you design and improve student assessment
You need to consider some of learning obstacles that might emerge
So you can plan ahead to mitigate how you would remove them.

In the process of engaging with others to develop an emerging technology, learners will face a myriad of individual and team challenges, problems-to-solve, and obstacles. Many of these obstacles can be anticipated. This chapter proposes some common ones that may emerge, to inspire you to plot ones that may surface when you teach and develop a mitigation plan.

Scrum in Agile production environments has a purpose beyond just being a tool for teams to update one another. Part of the goal of Scrum is for team members to communicate obstacles or 'blockers' they might have to see who on the team might be able to help remove those impediments. When designing a PjBL course, anticipate and plan for obstacles to get in the way of learners achieving your designed learning outcomes. This is because learners will be in unfamiliar waters when they go through a typical project-based course. Some common obstacles will be highlighted here followed by possible solutions.

© Patrick Parra Pennefather 2022
P. Parra Pennefather, *Mentoring Digital Media Projects*,
https://doi.org/10.1007/978-1-4842-8798-9

Obstacle: Learners have difficulty understanding how they are doing in the course because they don't have a reference point in their previous experience that they can point to. They are also not used to the metrics you will likely design.

Mitigation(s): Coming up with short and simple rubrics for assignments in addition to the final project and participation criteria all communicated in the first class will go a long way in easing their minds. In addition, a midterm evaluation will at least act as a barometer of how they are doing and providing them guidance with how they can improve their grade in the second half of the course will help them set goals.

Obstacle: Learners are used to discipline-specific rubrics and may find it difficult to receive any assessment without clear criteria.

Mitigation(s): If you are unsure, then you can use an assignment as a test of your criteria and receive feedback from learners as to whether the criteria were clear enough. This transparent approach, while unfamiliar to most learners, will establish trust and create a more collaborative learning experience.

Obstacle: Learners are not used to the idea of failing fast and will resist the concept.

Mitigation(s): At times it's better to avoid the word "failure" and "failing" unless you really describe what it means in the concept of iterative design. Walking learners through this instead of expecting them to know what you mean is key in clearing any confusion and resistance. You can reinforce this by including criteria in your rubrics that have something to do with risk-taking. You can prepare them for this when you reward their efforts in early assignments vs. the quality of the submission. Transforming every artifact they submit to you as a prototype will also keep establishing the relationship between prototypes, iterative design, risk, and the value of taking a risk over failing. Lastly, coming up with use cases in real-world designs that demonstrated failure-turned-success stories unexpectedly will further show the relationship between failing fast and innovation.

Obstacle: Learners will develop confidence the more they receive peer feedback and your feedback on their prototypes but anticipate that some may not want to speak up because of a concern that what they say may not be the right thing, because they have limited experience to base their insights on.

Mitigation(s): Encouraging learners to give each other feedback may take you the entire course to pull off. What's important is to elicit responses from those who are generally quiet. You'll likely be surprised at the insights they share, which for whatever reason they don't usually do so. This likely has to do with a lack of confidence in trying to grasp course content and processes they are just learning about. Address that early and you'll probably begin to receive more hands up with learners wanting to increase their participation. That participation is also effectively tied into their participation grade so they may on occasion need gentle reminders that they will need to summon their courage and offer feedback even if they don't think it's the right feedback in the moment. Of course, there are multiple ways to give feedback, and the use of chat threads on video conferencing applications has shown us that some learners prefer this way of communicating. There's nothing wrong with that unless you are conducting an in-person session. If you are, then it will be helpful to provide learners with additional ways that they can provide feedback to one another.

Obstacle: User-testing is a persistent dilemma in project-based courses. The pool of potential participants is small, and there is often not enough time to gather participants because by the time the team knows what they will test, the period between that insight and the actual test might have passed.

Mitigation(s): Courses in post-secondary institutions can go through an ethics procedure to support students in conducting user-tests that involves human subjects. Unfortunately, unless you plan on teaching regularly, it is much easier to have all students enrolled in the course agree to act internal user-testers for one another's projects. The other option is to have a client partner run their own user-testing sessions. This may also take time and money that the client may not be willing to budget for. Ultimately, you need to temper the need to have unbiased and an abundant number of user-testers for a PjBL course. A strategy is to focus learners on user-testing core functionality as this will shift the focus to making the interface and designed human interactions easier to understand and use. Different types of research methods, such as observation, screen recording, and talk-aloud, will need to be taught.

Obstacle: Time will be your biggest obstacle. You will never have enough of it so plan on that. Learn to prioritize where you put your time and record the patterns. Doing so will help support you in improving your next version of the course. A key thing to remember is that the larger the class, the less time you will have to mentor or even provide sufficient one-on-one feedback to everybody.

Mitigation(s): Plan on designing peer review scenarios, presentations, and class assessment of each other's work, etc. All these efforts will save precious time. Peer reviews can be anonymous although just like Retrospectives much of the time they require facilitation because learners sometimes don't have enough vocabulary or production experience to be able to provide feedback that is always useful to a team. The team or individual receiving feedback can also be more strategic in terms of preparing for the type of feedback that would most benefit them. Preparing learners ahead of time to do this will go a long way toward a more impromptu approach that might take up necessary in-class minutes.

Index

A

GPSR Compliance
The European Union's (EU) General Product Safety Regulation (GPSR) is a set
of rules that requires consumer products to be safe and our obligations to
ensure this.

If you have any concerns about our products, you can contact us on

ProductSafety@springernature.com

In case Publisher is established outside the EU, the EU authorized
representative is:

Springer Nature Customer Service Center GmbH
Europaplatz 3
69115 Heidelberg, Germany

www.ingramcontent.com/pod-product-compliance
Lightning Source LLC
Chambersburg PA
CBHW071405050326
40689CB00010B/1757